DOUBLE
JEOPARDY

DOUBLE JEOPARDY

Women Who Kill in Victorian Fiction

VIRGINIA B. MORRIS

THE UNIVERSITY PRESS OF KENTUCKY

Frontispiece: Depictions of a woman's violence were unusual in Victorian fiction. This illustration showing an elegant and determined Dark Lady in the act of shooting Charles Augustus Milverton was a dramatic exception. *Strand Magazine*, 1904.

Copyright © 1990 by the University Press of Kentucky
Scholarly publisher for the Commonwealth,
serving Bellarmine College, Berea College, Centre
College of Kentucky, Eastern Kentucky University,
The Filson Club, Georgetown College, Kentucky
Historical Society, Kentucky State University,
Morehead State University, Murray State University,
Northern Kentucky University, Transylvania University,
University of Kentucky, University of Louisville,
and Western Kentucky University.

Editorial and Sales Offices: Lexington, Kentucky 40506-0336

Library of Congress Cataloging-in-Publication Data

Morris, Virginia B.
    Double jeopardy : women who kill in Victorian fiction / Virginia
B. Morris.
        p.   cm.
    Includes bibliographical references.
    ISBN 0-8131-1751-8
    1. English fiction—19th century—History and criticism. 2. Women
murders—Public opinion—Great Britain—History—19th century.
3. Detective and mystery stories, English—History and criticism.
4. Women murderers in literature. 5. Trials (Murder) in literature.
6. Murder in literature. I. Title.
PR878.W6M67   1990
823'.809352042—dc20   90-32879

This book is printed on acid-free paper meeting
the requirements of the American National Standard
for Permanence of Paper for Printed Library Materials.
∞

For Ken

CONTENTS

ACKNOWLEDGMENTS

My interdisciplinary interest in criminal justice and literature, which engendered the idea for this book, evolved from teaching at John Jay College of Criminal Justice. The enthusiasm of my literature students, the encouragement of my colleagues, and the financial assistance of the Research Foundation of the City University of New York sustained my commitment during the research and writing. I owe special thanks to Professor Robert Crozier, Elisabeth Gitter, Patricia Licklider, Barbara Odabashian, and Robert Pinckert.

The Women's Division of the American Society of Criminology has welcomed my participation in its multidisciplinary analysis of the subject of women and crime, and many Division members have generously shared their particular expertise. I have been enormously enriched by that association and I am grateful for it.

I would like to acknowledge the indispensable critical response of those anonymous readers who saw the evolving manuscript. Much of its strength is the result of their comments.

To Karen Halloran and Jane Driscoll, who put the first version on computer discs and then answered endless technical questions about how to work with them, my eternal thanks.

But without the boundless enthusiasm and merciless editing of my husband, Ken Morris, there would have been no chapters to type, no manuscript to read, no book to publish. To him, and to our daughters Courtenay and Mavis, I owe more than I can say.

INTRODUCTION

Twice Guilty:
The Double Jeopardy
of Women Who Kill

When women murdered in Victorian fiction, they struck home literally and metaphorically. Their victims were usually their husbands, lovers, or children; their crimes almost always occurred in a domestic setting. In committing murder, these otherwise ordinary women also struck hard at the cherished image of Victorian womanhood—the gentle, nurturing guardian of morality and the home.

Violent crimes committed by women characters focused new attention on the motives for these desperate and unexpected acts. Even the most misogynistic reader had to acknowledge that women did not commit random murder. The simple equation linking unbridled sexuality to criminality did not explain the behavior novelists described any more than did dismissing guilty women as being too masculine.[1] Instead, women's economic and emotional dependence on men, and men's physical and psychological dominance over women contributed to, even precipitated, their one shocking moment of violence.

The books of manners and morals written for women—even those that acknowledged the discontent women had begun to express in the 1830s and 1840s—ignored the repressed, and therefore dangerous, rage of many Victorian women.[2] So did most of the fiction. But some English novelists who recognized the mounting tensions over the inequitable status of the sexes portrayed sympathetic criminal women in their fiction. In turn, the novels about violent women articulated a broad range of social problems that could, and did, lead to murder, problems that included discriminatory divorce legislation, men's physical abuse of their wives, and women's legal and economic subservience. There can be little doubt that the Victorian audience recognized the realism of the situations that the novelists described and the intolerable dilemma of the trapped woman even if they perceived each murderous action as the product of an isolated, individual moment of despair.

Mary S. Hartman observes in *Victorian Murderesses* that the events which prompted the rare real-life women to kill "display a pattern which suggests that, far from committing a set of isolated acts, the women may all have been responding to situations which to some degree were built into the lives of their more ordinary middle-class peers."[3] The same was true of the fiction. In an ironic inversion affirming the relationship of fiction to life, Rachel Brownstein, in the introduction to *Becoming a Heroine*, observes that some Victorian women killed their husbands because they were "enraged by life's failure to live up to romantic fictions."[4] Middle-class women in particular, she says, read "fictions" with formulaic treatments of love and courtship, with marriage as an inevitable happy ending. Sexual compatibility and physical domination were not discussed in romantic fiction, where the problems of married life received relatively little attention. Novels with women killers, on the other hand, examined the disparity between the ideal world described in the romantic fiction and the reality of women's marital experience. None of these fictional killers has a tolerable—let alone happy—marriage. Deprived of this measure of conventional success, the fictional woman's options were comparable to those of her real-life counterpart: she could suffer passively or find some assertive way to resolve her dilemma.

The overwhelming majority, both in life and in fiction, chose to accept their plight. If they tried to ameliorate their situation, they generally avoided personal retaliation either by leaving the abusive environment outright or using whatever legal means they could muster to resolve the dispute. Both of these approaches had serious practical limitations, however, because few women had alternative places to escape to and the laws tended to support the authority of men. But some of the mistreated women, if they were not physically or emotionally debilitated by their experiences, responded by attacking their abusers. Victims-turned-aggressors were, occasionally, subtly lauded for their courage; in some circumstances the criminal nature of their actions was overlooked, excused, or even glorified as striking a blow for liberation. Although no women killers in Victorian literature were transformed by their crimes into cultural heroines, almost all committed more or less justifiable homicide. But the self-contradiction which lay behind Victorian attitudes toward women's criminality, the dichotomy between women as morally superior to men and yet in every other way inferior to them, was not resolved even in the most thoughtful fiction.

One reason is that the novelists were not concerned with providing a broad overview of women's crimes (most of which were essentially petty) or even a representative sample of the murders women committed. Although crime is everywhere apparent in Victorian fiction, women are guilty—in the main— only of killing specific individuals directly tied to their personal or social oppression. Ignoring the dramatic potential of several gruesome real-life cases with multiple victims, and infrequently describing either suspected women who were not actually tried for murder or those who were tried and acquitted, the novelists concentrated on the ambiguous guilt and radical daring of women who chose to act for themselves. But as Victorian novelists described individual women capable and guilty of murder, they implied if they did not always explicitly state that the individual cases were part of a larger, legitimate gender battle—a power struggle between men and women—rather than simply individual examples of depravity or immorality.

Theoretical interest in crime and its causes also developed during the Victorian period, fostered at least in part by the awareness fiction had created of the fraud, corruption, and violence omnipresent in everyday life. Like the novelists, these historians and social scientists were more apt to write about criminal men than criminal women. When they did discuss women, they cited the same literary sources novelists did—Clytemnestra and Lady Macbeth, for instance—as exemplars of the evil women were capable of. But while they sought a more comprehensive assessment of criminality than the novelists, these writers were less progressive in their thinking. Few of them went beyond the idea that there was something wrong with a woman as a woman (that is, she had denied her nature) if she committed a violent crime. This may have resulted in part from the relatively small numbers of women killers in the criminal population (which made it easier to treat them as statistical aberrations) and in part from the overwhelmingly masculine bias in the scientific and academic communities. Furthermore, as the century progressed and the backlash sharpened against those women increasingly willing to demand certain rights and privileges, it was, ironically, scholars and researchers, claiming a disinterested and morally neutral commitment to truth and knowledge, who were most vitriolically opposed to treating women as men's equals.

Although my work is neither gynocritical in discussing only women's writing or gynetic in reassessing self, gender, and truth in western culture, it is feminist in its concentration on violent women characters and their role in Victorian fiction.[5] It describes how women, in particular deviant women, are defined within a particular time and place and how that definition has evolved and influenced western perceptions of women—deviant and not—until the present. It treats gender, class, and ethnicity as primary components of a literary character and explains how the balance among the three shifted during the century to make gender tensions and socially imposed gender roles a key explanation for violent behavior.

I have included men as well as women writers; the determining factor in each case was the extent to which a novelist developed women's capacity for violent behavior. For that reason Charles Dickens and Wilkie Collins are discussed in depth but Thackeray and Trollope are not. Similarly George Eliot and Mary Elizabeth Braddon are central subjects but the Brontës are not. My intention is to uncover a pattern of thinking about women who commit murder or come so close to it that they feel guilty of it all the same. Increasingly, my assessment shows, there is an incremental movement toward seeing violent women as justified agents of change, however brief their success in altering the inequitable balance of power which oppresses them. This view differs significantly from earlier, non-feminist readings such as Dorothy Van Ghent's or John Reed's. Reed, for example, in *Victorian Conventions*, contends that women characters who killed men were not only breaking the law, they were self-destructive. Their violence was evidence of their failure as women, of their "incompleteness and disharmony." Aggression made them miserable, he says, because there could be no credible excuse for such outrageous behavior.[6]

I propose to show that just the opposite is true. Their behavior resulted from the abuse they suffered at the hands of the men they killed. The dilemma the writers created for themselves is this: in explaining the women's motives and in making the women sympathetic, there is a latent advocacy of violence and law-breaking. While the novelists were sympathetic, they were also Victorians; they could not allow women to get away with murder or destroy the established power structure. As a result, guilty women did not benefit from their crimes by finding happiness or peace. When novelists did not subject the women to the jurisdiction of the courts, they made them commit suicide, withdraw from society, or become insane. The novelists thus insured that women could not escape the constriction of gender-role expectations. What that means, specifically, is that their crimes were portrayed as the consequence of sexual or intellectual independence. It was that flouting of conventional decorum and subservience which put women outside the pale, doubly damned, rather than their justifiable homicides.

After describing the literary tradition of criminal women in chapter 1 and the legal position of Victorian women in chapter 2, I have organized the book chronologically, to show that attitudes toward women criminals evolved throughout the Victorian period, both for individual authors and the literary establishment as a whole. Most striking is the increasing frequency of, and the increasing justification for, women who murder abusive men and become agents of change rather than simply victims of aggression. Comparing Nancy's being beaten to death by Bill Sikes (*Oliver Twist*, 1837) with Tess Durbeyfield stabbing Alec d'Urberville (*Tess of the d'Urbervilles*, 1894) makes the point.

While it is difficult to prove conclusively that the authors borrowed from each other, careful reading of the texts demonstrates that a change took place in the treatment of women criminals in both popular and more serious fiction. I have examined both, not only because both include women killers but because any comprehensive account of changing cultural and literary attitudes demands it. Victorian scholarship has already demonstrated the validity of that approach.[7] Also the fact that so much popular fiction involving women criminals was written by women for women would, in any event, validate its inclusion.

As women became more and more the subject of fiction, more issues directly related to women came into literary focus. Since women had been conceded power in the domestic sphere, private issues like abusive treatment, family planning, and economic dependence assumed greater importance in fiction about women. Many of the women created by the novelists used subversion to fight male authority. But women who kill do not subvert masculine control; they assault it. Novelists describing such assaults assumed that the imbalance of power was culturally imposed, not natural or innate, and was bound to change. Yet all of them, as this book will show, had internalized the legal and moral values of a culture which insisted that it was wrong to kill and that it was especially wrong for women to kill. The fiction, then, portrays murdering women as active agents and sympathetic criminals, yet yields to the ideologies which in Judith Newton's words "sustain and legitimate the power of the male bourgeoisie in relation to society as a whole."[8]

Both feminist and interdisciplinary, the book is set firmly within a historical context—the nineteenth-century debate on "the woman question." By focusing on women who kill in Victorian fiction, it provides a new perspective on characters who might otherwise have little in common and a new reading of what the novelists were saying about women's violence. For while Victorian fiction was topical, most novelists were doing more than mirroring the world they lived in. Some, whether they intended to or not, perpetuated the stereotype of the woman killer as over-sexed and over-emotional. Others increasingly provoked their readers to reassess their perceptions of women criminals, and in doing so helped to transform the image of women's nature from passivity to active involvement. Their women characters served, in other words, as transitional figures between the idealized view of their sex and the representation of the experiences women actually had.

ONE

The Worst of Women: Sisters in Crime

In creating characters who break the law and suffer for it, writers have articulated a society's discomfort with crime and affirmed its expectation of punishment. Yet at the same time, the recurrent emphasis on the lawbreakers themselves stresses the fascination they, and their deviant behavior, hold for readers. More often than not criminals are the subjects, the protagonists, the heroes of literature. If they kill, however, their culpability is characteristically made somehow ambiguous. The western literary tradition that extends from Greek and Hebraic civilization to the twentieth century deems killing another human wrong and demands recompense. But victim, motive, circumstance, and even weapon can alter the crime and influence the assessment of guilt.

When the killers are women, their crimes violate more than the legal code and the underlying ethical norms, and their guilt is judged differently. The biblical Judith, Aeschylus's obsessively revengeful Clytemnestra, Shakespeare's politically ambitious Lady Macbeth, Webster's passion-driven Vittoria Corombona, and their fictional sisters in crime, all commit bloody acts. Yet unlike men, for whom violence can represent proof of masculinity, violence in women has almost always been understood as aberrant and self-destructive.[1] Women guilty of violent crime are at odds with the culturally nurtured image of acceptable womanly behavior, and they are punished as much for this violation as for the actual crime they commit.

The archetypal murders committed by women in Greek tragedy and biblical narrative are acts of revenge and retribution. Clytemnestra's stabbing of her husband Agamemnon in Aeschylus's tragedy, for example, grows out of her compulsion to avenge his sacrifice of their daughter and her rage at his flaunting of Cassandra as his war prize. But however compelling Clytemnestra's motives, however just Agamemnon's fate, their son Orestes kills her in retribution—for his father's death and for her flagrant adultery. The requisite destruction of assertive, violent, sensual women, ingrained as a theme in western literary tradition, is reaffirmed in *The Eumenides*, the final play in the trilogy. There the justice of the state, fairer than the justice of revenge, protects Orestes from the price of matricide although it was not invoked to save Clytemnestra.

Euripides' *Medea* takes a different, yet not totally antithetical, approach to the causes and consequences of female violence. When Medea is rejected by Jason, a man with more political power than she has but less strength of character, she too chooses murder as the means of retribution. But rather than attacking her adversary outright, she kills his new bride and her own sons. On the face of it, her crime is even more horrendous than Clytemnestra's because her victims are helpless and guiltless. Indeed, infanticide and the destructive rage of betrayed passion have been associated with Medea's name in western literature ever since. Yet unlike Clytemnestra, she is rescued by divine intervention before she can be arrested, with no further punishment than the loss of her husband and the death of her children.

In both cases, a woman's violent actions are portrayed as unusual and shocking, rather than typical of a pattern of aggressive behavior, even though Medea as a non-Greek with a past history of violence might have been judged by a different standard. Furthermore, the dramatists suggest that unusual circumstances drive the women to act in ways inconsistent with their natures, even if they are by nature strong and self-confident. This tacit acknowledgment that women are only spo-

Eugène Delarcroix emphasizes Medea's desperate vulnerability rather than the revenge she seeks against her unfaithful husband by murdering their children. Courtesy of Culver Pictures.

radically aggressive, and thus only sporadically criminal, is a key component of the western literary tradition.

A third perspective on women's responsibility for the violent deaths of their enemies, real or perceived, is found in Euripides' *Hippolytus*. Guilty of a secret yet passionate obsession with Hippolytus, mortified that he knows of her passion, and fearful he will betray her to her husband, Phaedra leaves a suicide note falsely accusing her stepson of assaulting her. As she expects, Hippolytus is cursed by his father Theseus and then, unexpectedly, killed by his grandfather Poseidon. Because Phaedra has already killed herself, only her reputation is left to suffer, and it does. Her name has become synonymous with licentiousness— though she was in fact chaste. Like Clytemnestra, her motive is linked to guilty sexuality, a key component in the Greek conceptualization of women killers. I think it no coincidence that Medea, the one who does not die for her crimes, loves only her husband.

When a woman's passion or her demeaned self-worth is not offered as a motive for her crime, she is sometimes portrayed as usurping masculine authority and thus deviating from her proper gender role. The biblical Judith, who rescues her nation singlehandedly by cutting off the head of Nebuchadnezzar's commander-in-chief, Holophernes, is an early (and uniquely positive) exemplar of this model. Disgusted with the defeatist attitude of her countrymen and devoted to the sovereignty of her God, Judith devises her own solution to the siege of Bethulia and insists that the city fathers help her. At a loss for alternatives and in awe of her determination, they agree. Her plan, never shared with the elders and only gradually revealed to the audience, is brilliant; it puts her in the perfect position to kill and escape unscathed.

Judith is different from other biblical women responsible for men's deaths, like decadent Jezebel (1 Kings 16-21), quick-thinking Yael, who drove a tent peg through the brain of an enemy general (Judges 4, 5), and agonized Tamar (2 Samuel 13), whose rape and rejection by her brother Amnon incited her brother Absalom to revenge and murder. Judith deliberately uses her beauty as bait and her powers of deception as a trap.

Tardieu's engraving illustrates the nineteenth-century transformation of Judith's reputation from Old Testament heroine to bloodthirsty and arrogant predator. Courtesy of Culver Pictures.

She prizes her honor and does nothing to compromise it, but she allows Holophernes's men to assume he has seduced her. The language she uses as she asks God to bless her plan makes her intention clear: "Use the deceit upon my lips to strike them dead . . . [and] shatter their pride by a woman's hand. . . . Grant that my deceitful words may wound and bruise them" (*Judith* 9: 10,13).

In the biblical story, public reaction to Judith's victory (and even to her rather ghoulish decision to take the general's severed head back to her people so they can terrify his leaderless troops with it) is euphoric praise and profound respect. When the Assyrian army retreats in disarray, Judith is acclaimed the "heroine of Israel" and the "glory of Jerusalem," the savior of her people. But Victorian images of her are less flattering, equating women's potential for criminality with deception and trickery. For them, Judith was a precursor of Salome (Matthew 14), who was prompted by her mother to ask for John the Baptist's head as her reward for pleasing Herod with her dancing and evolved in Christian culture into an archetype of erotic and destructive womankind.

These women characters, sometimes protagonist, sometimes criminal, and sometimes both at the same time, shaped Anglo-American conceptions of violent women from the Renaissance through the Victorian period and beyond. Though appearing in different literary traditions, they embody three subsequently reinforced views: violent crime is unusual, even unnatural, in a woman; it is often the result of intense sexual passion; and it depends on deception or deceit for its success. English Renaissance dramatists emphasize these points when they include women killers as characters in their tragedies. Shakespeare, Webster, Beaumont and Fletcher, and the trio of Ford, Rowley, and Dekker create passionate women who wield daggers or dispense poison although women are less commonly violent than men and more often incite others to do the crime they advocate.

Lady Macbeth, although she does not commit murder herself, incites her faltering husband to kill Duncan. She accepts the necessity of murder to make her husband king of Scotland before

Macbeth does, and she suborns her womanly nature to make herself capable of violence:

> Come, come you spirits
> That tend on mortal thought, unsex me here;
> And fill me, from the crown to toe, top-full
> Of direst cruelty! Make thick my blood,
> Stop up the access and passage of remorse;
> That no compunctious visitings of nature
> Shake my fell purpose, nor keep peace between
> The effect, and it! Come to my woman's breasts,
> And take my milk for gall. . . . [act 1, sc. 5, lines 41-49]

In that way, Lady Macbeth differs from most classical archetypes and from Shakespeare's other violent women because her crime is not linked to sexual passion; nor does she use sexuality deceitfully to further her schemes. Rather, to make herself capable of murder she rejects her sexual identity and, by implication, becomes more man-like. However, her determination to rid herself of feminine weakness cannot save her from the consequence of unwomanly violence: obsessed with the murder she forces her husband to commit, and unable to accept her own urge to violence, she goes mad—as she predicts she will. Her madness and ensuing suicide are critical to Shakespeare's characterization of the woman criminal as unable to benefit from unnatural violence. Victorian authors seized on the idea that a woman is unable to profit from her criminal deeds because she is psychologically and morally unable to accept the consequences of her deviant behavior. This notion, as we will see, persists even in the novels where women's motives are much more sympathetic than Lady Macbeth's.

Goneril and Regan, in *King Lear*, are more shocking than Lady Macbeth and more revolting. Their initial violence, in addition to being directed against old men, has a quality of personal cruelty rarely equaled in literature. Particularly repulsive is their inability to feel the slightest remorse for their actions. They drive their father out into a wild storm and refuse to allow him any of the appurtenances of retired royalty. They

Lady Macbeth's frenzied urgency to have Duncan murdered despite her husband's dread dominates Fussli's vision, as it did the misogynistic Victorian imagination. Courtesy of the Tate Gallery, London, and Art Resource, New York.

debate Gloucester's punishment for being sympathetic to Lear, Regan urging that he be hanged and Goneril demanding that his eyes be plucked out. When the latter prevails, Regan encourages her husband in the old man's mutilation and dismisses the blinded Duke: "Go thrust him out at gates, and let him smell / His way to Dover" (act 3, sc. 7, line 93). By comparison, the fact that she stabs and kills the servant who has mortally wounded her husband seems a tolerable act of vengeance.

Perhaps because Regan and her husband have been allies in cruelty, her violence diminishes after his death, especially as she feels awakening sexual interest in Edmund, Gloucester's bastard. Goneril, on the other hand, grows crueler. Though her appalled husband curses her as demonic, he is reluctant, through misplaced chivalry, to interfere: "Howe'er thou art a fiend / A woman's shape does shield thee," he concedes (act 4, sc. 2, lines 66-67).

She grows more fiendish yet, poisoning her sister Regan, her rival for Edmund's affection. She shows her mortally wounded lover no sympathy, instead cursing his weakness: "Thou art not vanquished, / But cozen'd and beguil'd" (act 5, sc. 3, lines 153-54). Foiled in her ambitions to rule but arrogant to the end, she commits suicide by stabbing herself in the heart. She feels no remorse or repentance—she is all defiance and passion, and her actions forbid any possibility of a sympathetic reading. Goneril's sexual appetite, although not the only motive for her crimes, is inextricably wedded to her unnatural cruelty. That pattern dominates the conception of criminal women in John Webster's *The White Devil* (1612) and Beaumont and Fletcher's *The Maid's Tragedy* (1619), two Jacobean dramas where women are guilty of murder.

In Webster's play, Vittoria Corombona does not break her husband's neck or poison her lover's wife, and she only thinks she has shot her brother to death. But there is no question of her complicity; she incites her lover to commit the first two murders and extracts his vow of compliance, a vow he feels compelled to fulfill. She fully intends to kill her brother and fails only because he tricks her by carrying unloaded pistols. Her motive for all of this bloodshed is lust for the profligate life she adores; she shows no more remorse dying than she had when warned of the consequences of her plotting. Rather, she wonders where death will take her soul, although Webster makes it clear her corrupted nature will find its natural home in hell.

For all her crimes, Corombona is a fascinating character, true in her own way to her lover and full of zest for a more interesting life. Though Webster is brutal in his characterization, asserting that "were there a second Paradise to lose, this devil would betray it," she is never inhuman and so not totally repulsive. And while the conventional ending of a blood tragedy demands that the stage be littered with bodies, one is tempted to imagine that Corombona came as close as anyone to getting away with murder. She, like Goneril and Regan, helps to establish the traditional correlation of sexual excess and female criminality, though few of the women killers in later English literature share her zest for sin.

Beaumont and Fletcher's Evadne is an adulteress who avenges her husband's honor and her own by stabbing her royal lover to death in *The Maid's Tragedy*. Although her story has some superficial similarity to Corombona's, its moral is more complex. Evadne is no innocent led astray but a forthright and sensuous woman. When she refuses to sleep with her new bridegroom, she makes it clear that it is neither lack of desire nor will but her involvement with the king that keeps their marriage from consummation. And to the jealous king she is equally blunt:

> if your fortune
> Should throw you from this height, I bade you trust
> I would forsake you, and would bend to him
> That won your throne. I love with my ambition
> Not with my eyes. [act 3, sc. 1, lines 174-79]

Her eventual reformation, prompted by her brother's demand that she repent and avenge the family's reputation, combined with her realization that she has degraded herself, turns her into a champion of womanly honor: she confronts the king with his guilt and kills him for destroying her, leaving his servants marveling that a woman could be capable of such a deed. But she is only briefly a woman of great power; within moments the new king decides that the inspiration for the crime was masculine, not feminine, and goes looking for her brother. Nor will her husband forgive her, either for being the king's mistress or for killing his king. Because she cannot redeem herself in his eyes, she commits suicide.

When we consider the play as an antecedent of more modern treatments of violent women, the curses Evadne heaps upon herself, and her conclusion that she "can do no good, because a woman," are more significant than her self-serving sexuality. They underscore the priggish self-satisfaction of the men who believe that their honor is more important than hers and emphasize the irony and power of male approbation in a woman's life. There is no clearer illustration of the double jeopardy that violent women face than Evadne's dying for finally asserting her own value as a person.

One other explanation for female criminality evident in Renaissance drama, which eventually lost credibility in adult literature but persisted in fairy tales, casts the woman killer as a witch, possessed by the Devil and guilty of inciting heinous crimes. *The Witch of Edmonton* (1621) was the work of John Ford, William Rowley, and Thomas Dekker, a theatrical rendition of (or, depending on one's perspective, capitalization on) Elizabeth Sawyer's execution for witchcraft earlier the same year. The treatment of Mother Sawyer, though, is unusually sympathetic, as is the perspective on the potentially violent consequences of unhappy marriage, a theme with particular appeal to the Victorian novelists.

While she does, in fact, make a pact with the devil, Sawyer is driven to it by the frustration of being assaulted and abused by a particularly boorish and brutal citizen of Edmonton who incites the crowd against her.

> I am shunned [she laments]
> And hated like a sickness, made a scorn
> To all degrees and sexes. . . .
> Would some power, good or bad,
> Instruct me which way I might be revenged
> Upon this churl. . . .
> 'Tis all one
> To be a witch as to be counted one. [act 2, sc. 1, lines 132-
> 52]

In defending herself, Sawyer argues that manipulative women using their beauty, and men their money and power, cause much greater harm than any poor, reviled woman can do even if she is a witch. Finally betrayed by the devil as well, she goes to her execution defying her tormenters and unwilling to concede that she was the cause of murder or suicide. Her defiance is especially powerful because, despite the paraphernalia of witchcraft, her guilt is much less important than the lust, greed, and egregious cruelty of her adversaries.

Any direct link between Mother Sawyer and Victorian characterizations of guilty women is more tenuous than the influence of Clytemnestra or Lady Macbeth who were frequently cited by name; the realistic domestic environments in which Victorian women commited murder were not peopled by witches, and only very rarely by king's mistresses or duke's wives. On the other hand, besieged women who became violent were said to behave in "demonic" ways or were labeled criminals for actions which threatened the power structure, in much the same way that witches were blamed in pre-Enlightenment culture and even as late as Sir Walter Scott's depiction of Madge Wildflower in *The Heart of Midlothian* (1818). That other women joined the torture of Mother Sawyer also anticipates the later work; conventional women in Victorian fiction were only rarely supportive of women accused of violence or other crimes.[2]

The traditional dichotomy of woman as saint and as harlot so characteristic of medieval and Renaissance Christianity and so evident in these plays helped to reaffirm the convention that female deviance, including criminal behavior, was linked to assertive (and thus inappropriate) sexuality. Puritan moral rigidity and Cromwellian misogyny also intensified a growing literary tendency to define that criminality as rebellion against masculine authority. As Sandra Gilbert and Susan Gubar point out in *The Madwoman in the Attic*, one of the most powerful influences on the negative image of deviant women in the nineteenth century—both as they were portrayed in fiction and as they saw themselves—was John Milton's portrait of Eve in *Paradise Lost* (1667).[3] Eve is the woman whose appetite (especially her taste for equality and self-determination) engendered all our sorrows. The calamity she caused by being assertive and independent rather than diffident and subservient was Paradise lost and mankind doomed. Adam blames her, bitterly and repeatedly, for beguiling and destroying him even as he insists on her "frailty" as part of the "infirmer Sex" (book 10, line 956).

Her punishment, of life-long submissiveness and pain in childbirth, and her penitence are overshadowed—even trivialized—by the power her error engenders in Sin.[4] The offspring and lover of Satan, the mother and lover of Death, Sin grasps the opportunity Eve's fall offers to enthrall and "kill" men (book 10, line 402). This archetypically deceptive figure, even more graphically than Eve, emphasizes the connection of women's energy and passion with guilt and destruction. Enchantingly fair above the waist and hideous below, she needs no prompting to infect and destroy; rather, she takes pleasure in it. Nor can the archangel Michael's description of future salvation deny her persistence or success. As Milton knew all too well, the Resurrection did not defeat or eradicate Sin.

In *Samson Agonistes* (1671), Dalila's destructive, serpentine power is more human but no less threatening than Sin's. Nearly half the drama is spent rehearsing her treachery in betraying the secret of Samson's strength to his enemies after she has seduced him with tears, smiles, and other feminine wiles into telling her. Central to her blame is Milton's conviction that there are things men know which women should never learn. Although the poet makes Samson admit his complicity in telling her his secret, the blinded and chained hero makes excuses for his own vulnerability to Dalila's charms but will not forgive her for gaining and using the power she has had over him. Milton's insistence that unless women are subordinate to men, the men will be destroyed (lines 1046-60) is at the heart of his antifeminism. Validated by his vaunted reputation and enduring popularity, that stance was at the heart of the Victorian notion that men and women belonged in separate, unequal spheres.

During the eighteenth century a different attitude—actually several attitudes—toward women who violated laws and mores emerged, modifying but never completely overshadowing the Miltonic verses. Daniel Defoe's is the most innovative, although not the most enduring. His bawdy thief Moll Flanders is probably the best-natured criminal ever created (1720) and his Roxana (1724) the most successful sexual entrepreneur. Moll robbed, cheated, and married with great regularity and little regard for legality; a succinct picture of her picaresque adventures is suggested in Defoe's prefatory description: "Moll Flanders

. . . was born in Newgate, and during a life of continued variety, for three-score years, besides her childhood, was twelve years a whore, five times a wife (thereof once to her own brother), twelve years a Thief, eight years a transported felon in Virginia, at last grew rich, lived honest, and died a penitent."

Defoe is more ambivalent about Roxana, once an abused and abandoned wife, who markets her feminine charms with enormous skill and good humor. Although she seems rather silly and not very smart, she calculates each decision she makes to yield the greatest possible advantage and becomes enormously wealthy in turn. However, when one of her abandoned daughters is murdered to prevent Roxana's exposure as a bigamist and a high-priced whore, the lighthearted tone changes. Although she does not commit the crime herself, the loyalty she inspires in her alter ego, the serving woman Amy, compels the girl's death and prompts Roxana's remorse. Her actual responsibility for Amy's action remains ambiguous because of the narrative approach Defoe adopts in creating Roxana's character. Throughout she is candid and straightforward, never seeming to mask her thoughts. When she says a decision is self-serving, we believe her. Yet despite the angry objection she expresses each time Amy suggests murder, there is the persistent sense that she is guilty.

In part that is because the murder is premeditated; the women argue about it repeatedly over a period of weeks, Amy advocating it and Roxana forbidding it, both conscious that its purpose is to protect the mistress. Furthermore, the victim (although she is an astoundingly annoying person) is one of several children Roxana has abandoned without qualm. Had the enemy been her offending and offensive husband, Roxana would have felt no guilt, but her responsibility for her children nags her. And when Amy disappears, "resolv'd to take her own Measures, without consulting . . . any-more,"[5] Roxana worries only about the servant, ignoring the implicit threat to the girl. Yet faced with the truth, she becomes sentimental—even maudlin—about her poor child and vows to kill Amy herself in retribution. By leaving the impression, at the hurried and inconclusive ending of the novel, that Roxana suffered for the child's death, Defoe invites or permits the reader to assume his heroine's complicity.

But except for that moment, the novelist's coupling of legal peccadilloes with the rowdy good humor that infuses his heroines and allows Moll, at least, her ultimate salvation jarred with the more serious view that novelists in the next century took of women who broke the law and thereby challenged the established balance of power.[6] What he offered, underneath the humor, was a biting indictment of a society that put women in the position of fending for themselves, often by fending off men. It seemed impossible, under those circumstances, to fault them for finding a way to cope.

A similar perspective is evident in John Gay's contemporaneous drama *The Beggar's Opera* (1728), and to a lesser extent in the characterizations of several minor women in the great novels of mid-century. The fully developed criminal characters were men, however, not women; and men were the primary criminals in the popular fiction of the late eighteenth and early nineteenth century generally described as Newgate Novels.[7] The plots and characters were drawn loosely from the details of actual cases reported in chronicles of crime like the Newgate Calendar (ca. 1773, 1824, 1826). Except for William Thackeray's *Catherine* (1839), which was intended as a satirical attack on the genre, women were more apt to be victims of crime than its perpetrators. But the novels raised provocative questions about guilt and punishment during a period when the country's criminal laws were undergoing radical reassessment, questions that later Victorian fiction wrestled to resolve.

The Gothic romance, with its supernatural trappings and bizarre twists of plot, also influenced the use of criminal themes in the realistic Victorian novel. Although the Gothic, like the crime novels, emphasized male criminality, there were a few predatory, destructive women like Matthew Lewis's Matilda (*The Monk*, 1796), Anne Radcliffe's Marchesa di Vivaldi (*The Italian*, 1797), and Charlotte Dacre's eponymous Zofloya (1806), whom Judith Wilt describes as "doubly Gothic." Not only are they responsible for murder, but they violate and degrade marriage, motherhood, and religious commitment. Nothing any realistic character might do could shock a reader who had read Walpole and his heirs—and most Victorians had. Wilt persuasively argues as well that describing marriage as murder, or as the milieu for murder, in the way George Eliot repeatedly does in her fiction is the legacy of the Gothic tradition.[8] The excesses of the genre, admittedly part of its appeal, ironically made the murderous women of more sober Victorian fiction credible— despite the scorn implicit in the voices of the Victorians when they used the epithet Gothic.

In realistic fiction, women's experiences with men provided, with few exceptions, the context if not the direct impetus for their violence. When a woman was willingly involved in an illicit sexual relationship (like Hetty Sorrel in George Eliot's *Adam Bede*), her culpability in any resulting crime of violence was unforgivable within her own social environment, although the author or the reader might take a different, more sympathetic, view. "Sexual appetite was considered one of the chief symptoms of moral insanity in women," Elaine Showalter comments in *A Literature of Their Own*. "It was subjected to severe sanctions and was regarded as abnormal or pathological."[9]

Women seduced into sexual relationships instead of actively seeking them were sometimes able to shed the taint of guilt. Elizabeth Hardwick, for example, describes women with sufficient strength of character and a "lack of mean calculation, of vindictiveness, of self-abasing weakness" to survive. For the strong (like the heroine of Mrs. Gaskell's *Ruth*), she asserts, "sexual transgression loses its overwhelming character as a wrong or a mistake."[10]

But a woman whose rage at betrayal, or at the social disgrace that sexual experience engenders, drives her to violent revenge faces a judgment more like that of the sexually aggressive woman. The Victorian novelists were not only members of a society at best unsympathetic and often openly hostile to unconventional women, but they were unable to disguise the threat to stability such women posed. As a result, few violent women are allowed to live after their crimes, and those who do are not restored to social grace. I believe that the tension between the idealization of sexual purity and the potential for bloody aggression which defines complex women in Victorian literature is created by writers willing to challenge convention but unable to dismantle it.[11]

Yet the one variety of guilty and threatening woman curiously under-represented in Victorian fiction was the femme fatale. This omission is particularly curious in light of the near-obsession that contemporary poetry, opera, and visual arts had with the subject, and in contrast to the frequency with which European novelists and playwrights created such women. But apart from Rider Haggard's popular novel *She*, Oscar Wilde's play *Salome*, and George Macdonald's *Lilith*, there are few women characters in British literature whose cold hearts and perverse desires make them persuasive threats to masculinity.

The reluctance of Victorian novelists to be sexually explicit, as any full-fledged treatment of the femme fatale demands, is hardly surprising. Mostly middle class themselves, they had internalized the cultural demand for decorum in literature that women and children would read. Their publishers, too, were reluctant to violate the deafening silence surrounding women's sexuality. Dickens, for example, explained in the preface to the 1841 edition of *Oliver Twist* that he felt obliged to spare his readers the explicit language and the sexual degradation that he knew were a part of the London underworld. Prostitution is never mentioned, let alone described; the reader is never told that the shame Nancy feels when she meets Rose Maylie is a consequence of her sexual experience. Similarly George Eliot and Thomas Hardy blur the details of their characters' sexual encounters, jolting a first-time reader into searching the texts for the moment when Hetty Sorrel and Tess Durbeyfield got pregnant. Yet in domesticating crime, in describing violence that occurred within a normal domestic environment, Victorian novelists rejected the idea that either sexual degeneracy or unnatural urges drove women to assault and murder.

Instead, Victorian fiction about criminal women showed women rebelling against their male-dominated lives and breaking away from restraints—familial and economic—which demeaned them. Their urgent need to seek revenge for sexual abuse and misuse put them in direct conflict with their society, especially with the men who customarily dominated them. Not content to subvert masculine authority the way many Victorian women did—the technique Judith Newton analyzes so perceptively in *Women, Power and Subversion*—they assaulted it head on. There were some other explanations for criminality, of course, just as there had been in the older literature: deception and deceit, bloodthirstiness, and greed often characterized the woman who broke the law. But the novelists repeatedly stressed the point that tensions between men and women were normal, and that when those tensions escalated, violence was often inevitable.

The assertive, aggressive actions of women who deliberately or passionately defy law and custom in order to avenge their plight grip the reader's imagination but perplex it as well. If they had been misled or misguided by their criminal lovers or husbands, they would be less troublesome, less disturbing to the conventional view that a woman's proper role is subservience to men. But they would also be much less interesting because they would offer less challenge to moral sensibility than the women whose crimes give them power—however fleeting—over their abusers.

TWO

Women and Victorian Law: A Curious Chivalry

Victorian women were exalted as morally superior but treated as legally, intellectually, psychologically, and biologically inferior to men. They were credited with shaping England's greatest achievements; their "decorum, respect, and propriety" were revered, in part to muffle agitation for real autonomy.[1] Yet they were unable to vote or to control their own property. In fact, until late in the century, married women had no legal identity apart from their husbands. The laws and traditions which relegated women to second-class status were defended—often vociferously—as the best way to protect them from anxiety and safeguard their special role as mothers and wives.

Women who challenged their separate and unequal status—either overtly by protesting against the most flagrant inequities or implicitly by defying conventional behavior—were abhorred as unwomanly and reviled as threats to established society. No women disturbed Victorian complacency more overtly than those who murdered. But despite their shocking behavior, most violent women were treated more delicately than men guilty of comparable crimes; they were acquitted more often, and their death sentences were more often commuted. The double standard, invoked, for once, to women's advantage, provided a cogent and ironic example of the Victorian dilemma: wanting to think of women as special, fragile creatures even when they did not act that way. While according to Havelock Ellis female criminality was more frequent in England than in other civilized countries, it is also true that women's violent crimes created a sense of dread out of all proportion to the actual threat they posed to society.[2]

By describing the frequency with which women killed, the targets of their violence, and the treatment they received from the criminal justice system, this chapter provides a historical context for the treatment of violent women in Victorian fiction. I am conscious that in describing "Victorian" ideas, or "Victorian" women, I am generalizing about complex subjects which changed significantly between 1837 and 1901 and encompassed seemingly self-contradictory positions. For instance, there is an unmistakable evolution toward parity with men in the adjudication of women's cases in the English courts. Yet the perceptions that violent women acted from individual rather than environmentally produced motives and that there was something wrong with them as women if they chose aggression rather than acquiescence run as constant themes through the journal articles, charges to juries, and crime histories of the century.

Murder was a popular topic in nineteenth-century England, in the inexpensive broadsheets, daily newspapers, and hastily assembled "true confessions" which reported murders in gross and gory detail. The unusual, the bizarre, the titillating were the object of popular fascination, as Richard Altick chronicles so thoroughly in *Victorian Studies in Scarlet*.[3] A middle-class woman's murder of her husband—probably because it happened so rarely—caused enormous public excitement. The standing-room-only crowd at her trial, packed with other middle-class women, revealed an insatiable curiosity about the details of the case. Since the presumptive motive in husband-murders was a wife's sexual indiscretions, they were doubly fascinating to a society also obsessed with sexual morality, especially the morality of women.

Similarly, domestic workers' violent crimes against their employers, because they highlighted the tensions implicit in class distinctions or exaggerated the vulnerability of the employers, received attention in the press disproportionate to their frequency. So did murders of patients committed by doctors and nurses. Most scandalous of all were the child-murders committed by mothers or mother-surrogates. Since a woman's role was so closely identified with nurturing children, the murder of a child was exploited as the most unnatural crime of all. Furthermore, the unidentified bodies of infants regularly discovered in the Thames (and other places) kept women's particular potential for violence in the public's consciousness.

Hoffer and Hull, in their study of infanticide, cite a Middlesex [London] coroner, Edwin Lankster, who reported that 22 percent of his inquests were on the bodies of murdered children. Another contemporary source claimed that between 1855 and 1860 there were 298 coroners' verdicts of willful murder against infants, or an average of sixty cases a year in metropolitan London alone. A third source put the figure at five thousand inquests nationwide.[4] The explanation for this shocking and depressing situation is all too simple: child murder was one way for an unmarried mother to avoid the disgrace imposed by the rigid moral code of the middle class and the related difficulty in obtaining domestic work. Similarly, factory work meant long hours and required the mother to make child care arrangements. The New Poor Law, in trying to control public welfare expenditures, inadvertently added another contributory motive—albeit unintentionally. Unmarried women were made financially responsible for their children and subject to legal action if they did not make adequate provision; yet no law created or protected jobs to make that possible.

Victorian society did not officially identify women as a special category of criminal in the same way it had begun to separate juveniles from older felons. Although the women were listed separately in judicial statistics and jailed separately from men if they were convicted, a murder by a woman was the same crime as a murder by a man. The only exceptions were violent deaths of children less than a year old, which custom defined as a woman's crime, and, after 1861, the death of a child as the result of a self-induced abortion or the failure to provide for its safe delivery, by default a woman's crime but not a capital offense.[5]

Juries consistently acquitted mothers who were accused of

killing their infants and young children, probably because the idea of executing them for the crime was even more appalling than its commission. C.A. Fyffe, writing in *The Nineteenth Century*, argued that the law accusing these women of murder was obsolete and allowed to stand only because the public knew that the punishment was "inoperative."[6] Several members of the commission which studied capital punishment in 1864-65 were in favor of abolishing the death penalty in infanticide cases. By the time the revision of the criminal code was being debated in the 1880s, Mr. Justice Stephen, calling the penalty "intolerable," urged (with many others) that a woman who killed a child under one year old should not be charged with a capital offense and suggested that judges use their discretion not to hold such women accountable for murder.[7]

Although the definition of infanticide which legally distinguished it from murder was not adopted until 1922, the mental unbalance accompanying postnatal depression was long acknowledged as a contributory factor in such crimes. Elizabeth Wolstenholme-Elmy, an articulate advocate of women's legal rights, expressed the situation as clearly as anyone. A new mother, and especially the young mother of an illegitimate child, is in emotional turmoil "which makes her for the time, scarcely a moral or accountable agent. [As] the crime is almost always committed under circumstances of sheer desperation, it is unjust to place such an offence on a level with ordinary murder."[8]

While the majority increasingly agreed that infanticide was a special case, they were also comfortable with describing a woman who killed her child as mentally unstable or incompetent because that reaffirmed the justification for the legal subordination of women to their husbands which jurists as far back as Chief Justice Edward Coke assumed was inviolable, but which was increasingly being attacked as inequitable.[9]

Although the nineteenth-century arrest, judicial, and prison statistics (which were kept in voluminous detail after mid-century) are not reliable by modern standards, they are adequate to reveal a number of useful details. For example, most women who were arrested were accused of minor crimes: stealing to feed themselves and their families, picking pockets, begging, or disorderly conduct. Few were implicated in assaults or large-scale robberies, and then almost always as accomplices of their husbands or lovers. In general, they posed little threat to society and almost none to the middle and upper classes because their criminal activities were concentrated in the working-class environments or the slums where they lived.

Women who murdered were only a small proportion of the total number of women tried for all crimes, but murder was the one crime for which women's arrest rates came the closest to arrest rates for men.[10] Roughly speaking, women were apprehended about one-fifth as often as men for crimes in general, but between one-third and one-half as often for murder. Between 1855 and 1874, when detailed statistics are available, it was 40 percent. The annual totals of women tried for murder in that period, which ranged from twelve to forty-two, once exceeded the number of men arrested on similar charges.[11]

Yet in that same twenty-year period, when, according to William Guy, 522 women were committed to trial for murder, only twelve (or 2 percent) were executed; extant records suggest another fifty-seven were reprieved after conviction.[12] That leaves 453 who were never indicted, or were acquitted, or sentenced to prison terms for lesser offenses, a large number of them for unpremeditated child murder. During the same period, 795 men were charged with murder, and 230 (or 29 percent) were executed. Women, in other words, were convicted less frequently than men in capital cases during those years and made up only a tiny proportion (5 percent) of the total executions. And between 1879 and 1888, when 154 convicts were hanged, only eight (again 5 percent) were women.[13] In the sixty-four years of Victoria's reign, women were convicted of about 15 percent of all murders and were executed at the average rate of just more than one per year. Women also made up about 15 percent of the total number after 1843, the first year in which the sex of executed persons was specified in official statistics.[14]

These statistics raise serious questions about what motivated the large number of acquittals and the decisions to commute sentences. It is clear, especially for women, that class was a critical factor in determining who would not be executed; middle-class women were not hanged, although several middle-class men were. Similarly, the nature of the crime was important. The more brutal and revolting the murder—the more unwom-anly—the more apt the perpetrator was to hang. Conversely, cases with compelling mitigating circumstances rarely resulted in execution. Millicent Fawcett argued, however, that the "good manners" which explained treating most women more gently than men only existed as a condition of subjection and that true equity before the law would have been a bigger gain for women's legal rights than this rather curious chivalry.[15]

Other gender-sensitive books and articles addressed the is-sues of criminal behavior and women's position under English law as well as providing discussions of individual trials with women defendants. The commentaries paralleled and often influ-enced the steady flow of legislation affecting women that was introduced into parliamentary debate after mid-century. Social reformers like Wolstenholme and John Stuart Mill, for instance, tied the criminal actions of women to injustices in the economic and social systems of the country, and particularly to women's lack of independence. Yet as environmental conditions gained increasing credence as the motive for men's crimes as the century matured, they were often overshadowed where women were concerned by the preoccupation with biological explanations for deviant behavior, a bias that women's advocates protested but could not change.

Some writers made serious attempts to analyze the traits that distinguished women criminals and to explain their punish-ments. As part of an exposé of the treatment of poor women driven to violence by abusive husbands, an article published in *The Echo* on 14 January 1869 pointed out that 37.2 percent of women prison inmates (and 33.3 percent of the men) were totally illiterate and argued that ignorance and poverty were linked as causes of crime. Another report in the same paper a few days later (19 January) compared the light sentence of one month in jail meted out to a "lady" shoplifter with the six-months of hard labor customary for working-class women convicted of the same

The insurmountable divide between a woman defendant and the male-dominated criminal justice system is dramatically conveyed in W.F. Yeames's "problem" painting. It provoked countless requests for the real story of the woman's crime. Courtesy of the City Art Gallery, Bristol, England.

crime; the writer was particularly dismayed that the lenient sentence was vehemently protested in the press as too harsh for a "lady."

From the other perspective, there were jocular treatments of pretty little women who were the cause of criminal havoc but little real crime and diatribes like Eliza Lynn Linton's attacks on the "new" liberated women as closet killers and patronesses of "charming young murderesses, adulteresses, [and] adventuresses."[16] And an articulate minority hammered away at the notion that criminal women were incorrigibly evil. One article from the *Bath Express* observed, in discussing Constance Kent's confession to murdering her young half-brother: "It was a wanton murder, not done by the hand of a man, for there is a *finesse* of cruelty about it that no man, we believe, however depraved, could have been guilty of; but it is the revengeful act of a woman—morbid, cruel, cunning—one in whom the worst of passions has received preternatural development, overpowering and absorbing the little good that she ever had in her nature."[17]

Longer studies of crime and criminals, especially the ones after mid-century written by Luke Owen Pike, Mary Carpenter, W.D. Morrison, and Havelock Ellis, generally included discussions of women criminals that attempted to analyze the frequency of their crimes, their personal characteristics, and their motives. Carpenter, one of the most perceptive and sympathetic, described the lost and degraded souls that populated the prisons and proposed some cogent reforms in their treatment. But she and the others were members of the middle and upper classes who considered the majority of criminals, both men and women, very different from themselves.

As a result, she stressed the ways in which criminal women were unlike most other women, abetting the idea that women who resorted to crime were by definition abnormal or unnatural. In addition, her work was limited by a nearly exclusive dependence on imprisoned convicts as the source of her information. Since the cases with the most repellent charges and those with the poorest defendants were most likely to end in long prison sentences, the sample was not representative of the women charged with murder or other serious crimes.

Because the police tended to be relatively lenient about arresting women except in the most outrageous cases or when long criminal records existed, and because the courts showed a similar reluctance to convict them, the relatively small number of women who ended up as prisoners—those whom Carpenter and others are talking about—were rebellious and recalcitrant, at least according to their warders. They were impervious to efforts to reform them into imitations of middle-class women or fit them for work as domestic servants, which was the general aim of the most enlightened and concerned prison officials. This small cadre of undeniably hardened women had a disproportionate influence on the perception that all women involved in crime were incorrigible.

In his chapter on women criminals, W.D. Morrison stresses the socialization of women as one of the reasons they commit fewer crimes, including serious crimes, than men even when they come from similar class and economic backgrounds. Although he concludes from this that women are more moral, he makes several observations which seem at odds with that explanation: working women, he says, commit more crimes because they have more opportunity; "the want of physical power" is a major impediment to women's success in crime and a major factor in their choice of weapon; and women are more apt to be recidivists (65.8 percent as opposed to 44.3 percent of men). The third point is in many ways the most revealing. "A plunge," Morrison says, "into crime is a more irreparable thing in a woman than in a man. A woman's past has a far worse effect on her future than a man's."[18]

And what of those women who committed violent crimes? Historical records reveal that like her modern counterpart, the Victorian woman killed intimate acquaintances or people dependent on her: husbands, lovers, children, wards, patients, and employers. But unlike twentieth-century women killers who use guns or knives—as men do—better than half of the documented Victorian cases were poisonings, frequently involving that old standby, arsenic. (Curiously, poison was rarely the weapon of choice in fiction—providing at least one example of art *not* imitating life.) Poison in general was relatively easy to acquire during the period, and arsenic in particular was used for many non-criminal purposes, including medicinal and cosmetic ones. Its chief use, of course, was to cope with the constant problem of rats and other vermin. From the killer's perspective, poison was a convenient weapon, as no force or violence was required and the intended victim, unaware of the threat, was unlikely to struggle.

Furthermore, a poisoning murder stood a good chance of escaping detection unless very suspicious circumstances surrounded the death, or other evidence attracted police attention. When the accused was poor, the suspicion was often based on a repeated attempt to collect insurance money; that meant, of course, that several unexpected deaths had already been noted by the insurer or the police. When she was from the middle or upper class, suspicion was generally aroused by sexual misconduct, specifically adultery. The five affluent women accused of poisoning deaths during the period (Madeleine Smith in 1857, Florence Bravo in 1876, Adelaide Bartlett in 1886, Florence Maybrick in 1889, and Edith Carew in 1895) were all involved in premarital or extramarital sexual relationships that became the focus of scandalous attention because the women were suspected of murder. The popular—and judicial—assumption in each case was that the accused had poisoned the inconvenient husband or lover in order to pursue her profligate sexual desires. The court and the press expressed the appropriate outrage, as the trial records, newspapers, and magazines of the period clearly indicate. Yet Bravo was not indicted; Smith's case was "Not Proven"; Bartlett was acquitted; and although Maybrick and Carew were convicted, neither was executed.

Despite society's reluctance to admit it, the motives which most frequently propelled working-class women to crimes of all sorts, including murder, were economic. In several well-publicized cases, which aroused more indignation than sympathy in the press and in the jury box, the prosecution claimed that the chief motive for murder was to collect insurance or burial fees. In other instances, elderly relatives, lodgers, or patients were killed for the small amounts of money they hoarded. While the paltry sums involved might suggest that the women were incredibly greedy or depraved, taking such desperate measures for so little gain meant rather that lives were cheap and survival very dear.

The most frequent crime of violence committed by impoverished women was child-murder, especially the murder of infants, an undeniable consequence of both poverty and the power of middle-class morality which denied the needy mothers domestic employment. Because the social stigma of illegitimacy and the resulting economic sanctions got stronger, not weaker, later in the century, women responded by asserting their own right of survival above that of their babies. In addition to the cases tried in the courts, there were hundreds where no indictments were possible because the identity of the murdered child and therefore her mother were unknown.

Particularly shocking, then as now, were instances of mass

child-murder often associated with the abysmal, money-making practice of baby-farming, or taking in children to board. New mothers paid a one-time fee to women (or couples) who boarded children until they could be "adopted." Instead of being placed with adoptive parents, the babies were disposed of, generally by suffocation, drowning, or starvation. Because many of the children were malnourished and ill in any case, deliberate murder of these abandoned infants and young children was hard to prove. Nor were their deaths a police priority.

But several notorious cases demonstrated beyond question that children were systematically murdered for profit. The cases of Margaret Waters (1870), Ada Williams (1899), and Amelia Sach and Annie Walters (1903) riveted public outrage on the perpetrators and probably more significantly on the need to reform the practice of informal adoptions which allowed such things to happen. The social and economic pressures which drove women to use baby-farmers in the first place were much less frequently blamed for the deaths, and there seems to be no case in which a natural mother was charged with murder for leaving her child with someone who caused its death.

Another direct motive for the domestic murders committed by working-class and impoverished women was linked to the physical abuse of women endemic in that male-dominated society. Husbands and lovers in particular, but also parents and employers, battered these women. In fact, until 1853, husbands were legally entitled to use violence and physical restraint to keep their wives obedient.[19] Such abuse reached epidemic proportions in impoverished inner cities—nowhere more dramatically portrayed than in the melodramatic but terrifying scene from Dickens's *Oliver Twist* where Bill Sikes beats Nancy to death (chap. 47).

Although the motives of the initial assaults were often complex—including such varied factors as alcoholism, repressive living conditions, financial frustrations, and social conditioning—the abused women had few alternatives for avoiding future confrontations. The most extreme, but also the most effective, was to kill the abuser. Several individual cases publicized in the press aroused enormous public sympathy for the accused woman and corresponding outrage at the abuse which had precipitated the murder. The *Times*, in a typical article in August 1872, protested judicial response to the abuse of women, arguing that recent trials revealed indifference to the maltreatment of women by sentencing abusive men to very short prison terms.[20] Perhaps as a result of the perception that women were frequently abused, cases in which women murdered abusive husbands were not always taken to trial after mid-century, and convictions rarely ended in execution unless the crime had been clearly premeditated.

Interestingly enough, self-defense pleas seem to have been invoked only rarely by women tried for murdering their husbands, although the so-called private defense provision of the law explicitly allowed a person being assaulted to kill an assailant in self-protection or to prevent the commission of a felony. The law specifically included assaults within a person's home as ones which could be met with justifiable violence. On the other hand, the law was expressed in masculine terms; it was what a reasonable man judged to be a threat to his person or property that qualified as self-defense. Cases used to illustrate various circumstances under which such a defense would be valid all featured men. Discussions of rape, for example, did not include any mention of legitimate self-defense by the victim although the assumption of Victorian law was that rape victims would always be women. The congruence of a woman's perception of an "immediate and obvious" threat to her life or safety with the intentions of the law has not been resolved even late in the twentieth century, leaving women who kill abusive men at any time except the precise moment when they are assaulted without certain recourse to such a plea.[21]

Despite the prevalence of spouse abuse among the poor, physical battering was not restricted to the most impoverished classes. Consequently, preventing abuse or avenging it was one motive for assault and murder that cut across class lines. While fewer middle-class women were accused of murdering their husbands than poor women, most cases involving affluent women claimed response to persistent physical abuse as a primary defense. But wife abuse was not always taken seriously, despite the efforts of committed journalists and novelists to bring the problem to public attention. In the face of repeated acquittals of women desperate enough to murder their abusers, the popular press, and even some of the essayists generally sympathetic to women, expressed the traditional view that most women who were abused "asked for it" by not being good wives. Caroline S. Norton, who knew from bitter experience that women were abused freely, voiced bitter exception to such sentiments. No one, she protested, could deserve physical abuse equal to that she had suffered at the hands of her own well-to-do husband. In the 1870s, Frances Power Cobbe's articulate newspaper articles and journal essays spelled out the extent of wife abuse and backed up her claims with judicial statistics. She insisted that women had to be legally protected or the levels of retaliatory violence would only escalate.[22]

In fact, measured numerically, more men were convicted of murdering their wives than women of killing their husbands. Given the difference in physical strength and the inevitable consequence of endemic wife-abuse in Victorian England, that is hardly surprising. But looking at the same figures proportionately, it is clear that murdered—as opposed to murdering—husbands made up a much greater share of women's victims than wives did of men's.

In 1853 the first law against wife-beating was passed in Parliament, but since the penalties provided by the bill—whipping and short-term imprisonment—did nothing to ameliorate the drunkenness, poverty, and misogyny that were the causes of abuse and made no provision to prevent repeated attacks, little changed in consequence. Women continued to be mistreated at home and found the law virtually powerless to help them. Furthermore, they still had to combat the popular assumption that if women were better wives, they would have better husbands.

In 1878 Parliament finally passed legislation allowing physical abuse as grounds for legal separation, and created a mechanism for court orders of protection to restrain abusive men. The problem of physical abuse persisted, though, throughout the era, abetted at least in part by the sentiment so clearly articulated by John Milton and others that man was created as woman's master, and by comments like Herbert Spencer's that women admired power and characteristically preferred strong men who abused them to weaklings.[23] Cobbe insisted that the double standard implicit in these attitudes encouraged men to abuse and even kill their wives, but held women guilty of causing their own deaths if they provoked their husbands into hitting them. She went even further to deplore the fact that women accused of killing in self-defense or as an expression of accumulated rage were treated as more guilty than the men who had precipitated their violence by assaulting or threatening them.

Women were rarely charged with violent crimes committed outside the domestic sphere. Few women of any class were tried for murders committed during robberies, and none for political assassination. There were scattered cases of women murdering their rivals in love triangles, which is really just another variant of domestic discord, and infrequent instances of what would today be called serial killings. These last, typified by Mary Ann Cotton, who killed several husbands and numerous children over a period of years before she was caught in 1873, and by Catherine Wilson, a nurse who killed at least seven patients before her execution in 1864, carried domestic murder to unusual extremes. Both women were hanged, apparently to popular approval, and no subsequently uncovered evidence has provided any reason to question the government's case against them.

In those cases where married couples were implicated in murder, the wife (or mistress) was customarily charged with acting as an accessory, and then only if she had prior knowledge of the crime. The chivalric (and sexist) assumption that men forced reluctant women into crime was at the heart of this tradition. The practice, according to Mr. Justice Stephen, evolved in order to provide women with protection similar to the old "benefit of clergy" tradition which had excused first-time offenders from prosecution or excepted them from punishment. It became a topic of heated debate during parliamentary discussions on the revision of the criminal code in 1879 and 1880; the commissioners who had drafted the revisions recommended it be abolished. Women's rights advocates like Elizabeth Wol-

stenholme-Elmy applauded that position, not only because the
law had been inconsistently applied but because its abolition
would end the "legal fiction of a wife's absolute subordination
to her husband" and recognize a married woman as "a free and
responsible moral agent."[24] In fact, the provision was not
dropped until 1925.

Only a few rare cases resulted in the execution of a husband
and wife for murder; the Mannings' double hanging in 1849 can
be explained by a concatenation of details: Maria Manning's
foreign birth, her Catholicism, her adultery with the victim, her
husband's atypical and unchivalric insistence that she was responsible for planning and carrying out the murder, the indis-
putably economic motive for the crime, and the fact that she
used a gun rather than a more "womanly" weapon. Her rather
grand manner, unbecoming in someone who had begun life as
a lady's maid, probably did not help her case either. In a more
gruesome tale, Mary Ann Barry and her common-law husband
Edwin Bailey were executed in 1874 for the murder of their
year-old child, the last in their series of encounters with the
law. If nothing else, the murder illustrates the degree to which
poverty and alcoholism were, then as now, intimately involved
with violence.

Most often, the wives and mistresses of male criminals were
discounted as serious criminal threats, and the law did not
consider them culpable. A married woman who gave "aid and
comfort" to her husband and his accomplices was not an accessory to the crime, but a husband providing similar support for
his criminal wife was liable to prosecution. As Wolstenholme-
Elmy points out, the distinction between the two is logically
inconsistent, as is the presumption that "natural affection" is
valid only for married women. Additionally, Mary Carpenter
speculates that women were arrested much less frequently
because their men shielded them, from either a protective
instinct or more probably an economic one.[25] It gives an appro-
priately Victorian twist to the tradition of honor among thieves.

But while women seem to have been treated more gently by
the judicial establishment and arrested less often by the police
under most circumstances, those who did run afoul of the sys-

were sometimes judged harshly, highlighting the unresolved dilemmas of British justice. For one, Victorian writers frequently acknowledged that society did not know what to do with women who were convicted of crimes. A contemporary comment in the characteristically conservative, often reactionary *Saturday Review* articulated the problem society faced: "British chivalry objects to the public laying on of hands in the case of a woman, even when most recalcitrant and disobedient; more particularly if a small and fragile-looking woman."[26] One consequence of this deference was the Victorian reluctance (increasingly obvious after 1850) to hang women for capital offenses, including murder. Another was to entrench the idea that woman's culpability was different because she was physically different. But most important was the notion that women's crimes were different in kind, "naughty" or the by-product of insanity rather than either vicious or self-defensive.

Significantly, some of the brutal treatment reserved for women in earlier times had been abandoned. Burning at the stake was abolished in 1790 as a woman's punishment for treason and petty treason (i.e., murdering a husband). Hiding an illegitimate pregnancy was not considered presumptive proof of the intent to commit infanticide after 1803, and after 1817 women were no longer whipped in public for criminal offenses. Additional prohibitions were added during the nineteenth century. Pregnant women were no longer hanged and neither were girls under the age of eighteen. As I have already noted, in the rare instances when they were convicted, women were not executed for infanticide when the child was less than one year old—clearly a recognition that such murders generally took place under extreme emotional distress and often economic desperation.

For both men and women convicts, a number of other significant changes in the administration of justice occurred in the nineteenth century. Transportation to the colonies ended in the 1850s; for women in particular, who had regularly been transported for even minor offenses, that meant a much greater likelihood of imprisonment closer to home. Capital punishment lost ground as the primary punishment for felonies and was replaced by penal servitude in national prisons. After 1803 the number of capital offenses was reduced dramatically, from about two hundred to eight by 1826 and to four by 1861.[27] Only murder remained a capital crime which women were likely to commit, the others being treason, piracy, and violation of the Dockyards Protection Act. After 1868, all executions were private, within prison precincts, rather than public spectacles. But although they did not face certain death, the conditions under which all convicts were imprisoned were abysmal, and for women in particular there was no real effort to provide rehabilitation or useful job training. Much greater effort was expended, often fruitlessly, on reforming their manners and morals.

But Mary S. Hartman and others have suggested that prosecutors and judges became harsher on the women charged with crime as women became more assertive in other areas. Middle class women, especially women who broke the law, Hartman comments, "were being made into scapegoats by many who were frightened or resentful of the rapid social change whose signs were everywhere."[28] It seemed to make little difference that most women charged with murder or other serious crimes were not political activists and had, for the most part, benefited very little from the rights and privileges women had gained through legislative reform.

It is certainly relevant to the treatment of women defendants that men dominated the legal system throughout the century; all judges, lawyers, and jurors were men. So were all the members of Parliament. Wolstenholme-Elmy insisted that justice simply could not be done under those circumstances: "[Women] have never in the case of a criminal trial the protection of a jury of their peers—they are prosecuted or defended by men, tried by men, judged by men. Is it impossible that sex bias should ever work "injustice"? Does it not, at the very least, often lead to the forgetfulness or neglect of the most important considerations?"[29]

No women were admitted to the English bar until 1919; the first women sat on juries in the same year, having finally become eligible when they gained the right to vote. Even then there were no female High Court or circuit court judges.[30] Despite

Madeleine Smith is dwarfed by the dimensions of the courtroom and outnumbered by the men who sit in judgment on her. But she had the last word: a verdict of Not Proven ended her murder trial. Courtesy of Culver Pictures.

the fact that women like Victorians Caroline Norton and Barbara Leigh Smith Bodichon were extremely knowledgeable in the law, especially as it applied to women, they had no direct way to influence its practice. Herbert Mannheim concurs with their frustration, in his discussion of the history of criminology, when he links the male-dominated criminal justice systems of the nineteenth century to the skewed, yet persistent, definition of criminal behavior in women that has endured into the twentieth century.[31]

The theory and practice of Victorian criminal justice that linked legal and moral issues in judging the criminal offenses of both men and women and made conformity to the middle-class morality the basis of criminal law in fact imposed more stringent standards for women because it demanded sexual as well as social (or gender-role) conformity from them although it did not from men. By stressing malice and wickedness as the chief components of a criminal act and rejecting the pragmatic, and morally neutral, view that criminal law exists to hold an individual's desires in check against the demands of social order, the law itself could be used to validate different standards of behavior. Sir James Fitzjames Stephen, in his role as draftsman and codifier of the criminal law, argued that the notion of malice should be dropped from the definition of offenses, yet as a jurist he was flagrant in his disgust for the moral turpitude of the accused, especially when she was a woman. Nor was he the only one guilty of inconsistency.[32]

Had the less moralistic view prevailed, fewer distinctions in the treatment of men and women might have been apparent. But in English practice it was a woman's criminal nature (as evidenced by her sexual and gender deviance) rather than the nature of women's crimes that received most judicial attention. In that context, though, it is relevant to note that bias resulting from judging an accused person on the basis of sexual "deviance" was not restricted to women; homosexual men were judged on similar grounds after 1861.

One reason that women's moral failings were judged so harshly is that behind the paternalistic Victorian dogma that women were morally superior to men lay the age-old image of woman as wild or degraded or evil and therefore capable of the most awful deeds. H.L. Adam's assertions in *Women and Crime* are characteristic of a whole body of commentary, although the book itself has serious methodological weaknesses because it argues from general impressions rather than empirical evidence. Claiming that women lack will-power, moral consciousness, and self-control, Adam observes: "One of the most staggering and repugnant attributes . . . exhibited by bad women is their perfectly fiendish cruelty. It is all the more startling by being displayed by one who is supposed to be gentle by nature. It is certainly a matter for meditation that the cruellest forms of crime are invariably committed by women. Some of them indeed are so terrible, both in conception and execution, as scarcely to be credited to human agency."[33] Women, in other words, could be considered the worst criminals either on the grounds that they defied the Victorian notion of true womanhood or that they exemplified the ancient idea of woman's inherent evil—yet another variant of the discrimination that assertively rebellious women faced.

In practice, the higher standard of behavior which was expected of women belied the myth of judicial neutrality on which England prided itself. A woman, that is, was condemned as more degraded—and therefore more guilty—than a man convicted of the same crime because theoretically she should have behaved at a higher level. Susan Jacoby has observed that the double standard of morality is best understood "as a code ceding broader powers of action . . . to men than to women. Under the double standard, it is scarcely surprising that any act of revenge by a woman looms larger, in myth and reality, than a comparable act by a man."[34] Precisely the same is true of a double standard of justice.

One result was that women who were accused of violent crimes were branded as "unnatural" and "defective" women. In her pioneering study *Women, Crime and Criminology*, Carol Smart comments that women convicted under such a system "are doubly damned for not only are they legally sanctioned for their offenses, they are socially condemned for being biologically or sexually abnormal."[35] The abnormality, of course, was defined by male social theorists, jurists, and journalists when women's behavior disturbed and outraged them by undermining their belief in female passivity and morality and their faith in the stability of a wife/mother-centered family.

In order to understand how men and women could be judged differently when they were accused and tried for the same crimes in the same courts, one must look at some specifics of the system. Although Victorian police investigation, courtroom procedure, and forms of punishment resembled modern-day practices far more than they did the workings of English justice before the great reforms of the early nineteenth century, and despite continuing changes in procedure which provided greater balance between the rights of the accused and the authority of the state, English justice was vulnerable to class and gender bias.

Most individuals indicted on serious felony charges who pleaded innocent were tried before a judge and a jury made up of relatively prosperous men with a vested interest in the status quo. Pleas could not be bargained, although in some cases suspects implicated by the police did not face criminal prosecution because judges exercised considerable discretion in deciding what charges a defendant would face. Even so, a significant proportion of the trials—with both men and women defendants—ended in acquittal.[36] At least one writer explained that juries' perceptions were that the police witnesses were biased and should not be believed without corroborating evidence.[37]

In the nineteenth century there were public prosecutors rather than private ones, as there had been earlier. The result was more uniform prosecutions; yet contemporary writers as well as more recent students of the Victorian judicial process have pointed to the wildly disparate sentences imposed for similar crimes as one of the great weaknesses in the administration of justice in the last century. A venerable and uniquely English tradition, which persisted until passage of the Criminal Evidence Act in 1898, was that a defendant neither took the witness stand nor was cross-examined. It was a controversial practice which had originated to prevent self-incrimination but evolved, especially for women, into an impediment to justice. Judging a mute defendant threw greater weight on the nature and plausibility of the charge and the perceived character of the prisoner, evinced at least in part by how she dressed and whether she seemed remorseful and humble. Those cases in which women seemed the most aggressive or were accused of unusual moral turpitude were the most likely to result in conviction. To put it another way, judges were rather too willing to condemn an action because the agent appeared to them a cad, or in the cases involving a woman, because she did not appear to be a lady.

By the 1880s, the accused could read a statement to the court outlining the chief points of defense, although it did not become part of the official record. In at least one infamous case, a woman defendant—Florence Maybrick—made such a statement to explain her relationship to her dead husband and her brief extramarital affair. But her determination to clear her name was ineffective; even her own attorney felt her candor about her unhappy marriage probably contributed to her conviction.

The judge in the case was none other than Sir James Fitzjames Stephen, the outspoken advocate of morally neutral criminal laws. Yet his summation reveals a bias against the defendant so strongly expressed that the jury found her guilty after deliberating for less than half an hour. For example, in dismissing the defense claim that men and women are held to unfairly different standards of behavior, Mr. Justice Stephen remarked: "I shall say absolutely nothing upon that subject. It is not to the point. We have not to determine any moral question at all, but simply to look at the matter as it comes before us, and with reference to the well-known and well-established rules of conduct. There is one thing in this matter upon which there can be no doubt whatever; in fact, we have it now stated by Mrs. Maybrick herself, that she did . . . carry on an adulterous intercourse with this man Brierley."[38] He described Mrs. Maybrick as "guilty," accused her of telling "wicked falsehoods," and labelled her freely acknowledged "disgraceful" liaison the probable motive for the murder.[39]

In concluding he admonished the jury that they were not deciding a medical case turning on whether or not James Maybrick had died of arsenic, but rather a moral case in which their judgment should be based on their "knowledge of human nature" about a woman who, in Stephen's words, "had already inflicted a dreadful injury—an injury fatal to married life."[40] But a markedly different spirit prevailed outside the courtroom. Women, many of whom had been faithful observers at the trial, helped to galvanize public opinion behind Maybrick. Her supporters, both men and women, were successful in persuading the Home Secretary to recommend commutation of her sentence to life in prison. Since the roughly contemporaneous trial and execution of Mary Pearcey for the murder of her lover's wife and child did not excite a similar reaction, it is evident that certain details of the Maybrick case aroused public sympathy.

First of all, Maybrick was from the middle class, living in circumstances with which her supporters could identify. Probably more significantly, they saw her as a victim rather than as an aggressor even though she had been convicted of murder. This phenomenon, allied to recent criminological studies of victim-precipitated homicide committed by battered wives against their abusive husbands, distinguished Maybrick's case

from Pearcey's but linked her with many of the other controversial cases with women defendants during the century. And
clearly Mr. Justice Stephen's prejudices made an enormous
impression—so much so that in an 1895 biography his brother,
Sir Leslie Stephen, felt compelled to deny the charges of misogyny that hung over his conduct at the trial.[41] It also demonstrated that a woman's adultery assumed monumental
proportions in cases where she subsequently killed her husband.
Although liberated women like Caroline Norton maintained that
adultery was the same for men and women, few agreed with
her, reaffirming Dr. Samuel Johnson's opinion that an unchaste
woman was worse than a thief who steals a sheep because she
"transfers sheep and farm and all from the right owner." Johnson,
in fact, in comparing a licentious single woman to a married
one, says that the difference is "between simply taking a man's
purse, and murdering him first and then taking it."[42]

Since Mrs. Maybrick had been stymied in her efforts to
separate from her husband, the issue of divorce was also per-
tinent in the public's response to her conviction. Divorce remained expensive and hard to get even after the Matrimonial
Causes Act of 1857 (and its amendments in 1858 and 1884), and
the rules for men and women were prohibitively different. A
man could win a divorce if his wife committed adultery; a woman
seeking to end her marriage on similar grounds also had to
prove that her plight was "aggravated by desertion, cruelty,
rape, buggery, or bestiality" before her claim was valid.[43]
Furthermore, women who did divorce their husbands were
treated as social pariahs in most circles, even if they had been
totally without fault, and rarely were able to secure custody of
their children.

Medical evidence also played a controversial role in the Maybrick trial, highlighting the still ambiguous position of the expert
witnesses who were becoming increasingly important to both
defense and prosecution cases. The doctors and chemists who
were called to give evidence on the cause and time of death not
only disagreed with each other but seem to have been totally
misunderstood by the judge and ignored by the jury. But because
there was no official criminal appeals process in England until

Florence Maybrick's candid admission of adultery was the chief evidence that convicted her of murder. The blatant bias of the trial made this unconventional woman the focus of public controversy over the justice of British justice. Courtesy of Culver Pictures.

1907, the questions of law or fact could not be referred to a higher court. The Home Secretary had the power to recommend the commutation of individual sentences, as he did for Maybrick. Such action was taken from time to time, more frequently toward the end of the century than in the beginning and generally because the cases aroused enough public attention to pressure the Secretary to act.

Like Florence Maybrick, women spent years in penal servitude on murder convictions though they were often released sooner than men with comparable sentences, especially since most women guilty of murder were first offenders.[44] But as important as Maybrick's story is for explaining the disadvantages confronting women accused of violent crimes, her case was unique precisely because she was middle class.

Without question, social standing made a difference not only in women's treatment after arrest and conviction but in their vulnerability to arrest and prosecution and their ability to attract the kind of public interest that produced the outrage accompanying Maybrick's conviction. The masculine protectiveness—sometimes called the new chivalry—which guarded middle-class women not only from the opportunity to break the law but also from the consequences of having done so was simply unavailable to working-class or indigent women, who were considered inferior in all ways, including their proclivity for crime.

Although an influential early study of crime prepared by the Royal Commission on a Constabulary Force (1839) discredited the causal relationship between poverty and crime, that relationship was one frequently acknowledged by serious students of crime and criminals in the nineteenth century. But while most Victorians rejected the idea that an evil nature was the primary cause of crime, they substituted the idea of the existence of a degenerate criminal class as the major source of what they identified as a growing crime problem.[45] They believed that crime-promoting social conditions were aggravated by the disintegration of moral standards, in particular the moral standards that defined middle-class life and middle-class womanhood. While such a belief focused particular attention on the immoral behavior of working-class women, it is clear in retrospect that the opposite influence, of pernicious poverty undercutting the relevance of an alien (because middle-class) moral conformity, was the real cause.

Furthermore, middle- and upper-class women did not identify with the problems which often provoked the economically motivated crimes of the lower classes or with the women who committed them; in fact they were often vitriolic in their condemnation of the immorality of the accused. Even more to the point, middle- and upper-class men, like the ones who sat on the juries, ignored their responsibility for the economic situation of the poorest classes, including the abandoned mistresses and dismissed servants who committed desperate crimes and the illegitimate children who were sometimes their victims.

The laws governing penalties for seduction make the impact of class distinction inescapably clear. It was a felony to seduce an heiress, or even to marry her before she was twenty-one without her parents' consent, yet no crime at all to seduce any other girl over the age of thirteen. And this was true at a time when 75 percent of the illegitimate births annually were to girls younger than nineteen. Nor was there any legal requirement that the men who had fathered these children support them, although the mothers could be punished as disorderly and idle if the state had to support the children.[46] In the same vein, the Criminal Law Amendment Bill of 1885 defined rape as a felony only in cases of forced assaults, calling intercourse obtained by seduction, drugging, and similar means simply a misdemeanor.[47] In other words, the faults in the criminal justice system itself were confounded by legal discriminations against the women most apt to be defendants.

In addition to the general bias that laborers and the impoverished in general and poor women in particular were less moral than members of the middle class and therefore more prone to crime, lack of money directly influenced their inequitable treatment in the courts. After 1836, defendants secured the right to be represented by a lawyer, but if there was no money for a professional defense, the trial proceeded without one. The poor, and those who lacked the financial support of family and friends, were often denied access to qualified counsel—and consequently to a fair trial. While this obviously affected both men and women, a significant percentage of the women accused of killing their infants and husbands lacked personal or professional advocates. Having violated their moral responsibility as wives and mothers and forfeited the protection of their families, they were at even greater risk in the courtroom.

Mary Carpenter described some of the consequences for women found guilty of crime in *Our Convicts* (1864). She pointed out that imprisoned men came from many social classes, while women almost always were from the lowest, or in her words, the pariah class. Certainly they ended up as social outcasts, despite the socioeconomic position of their families. Furthermore, men punished for crime were able to maintain a degree of respectability, she observed, while women "were completely cut off from the honest and respectable portion of society, and therefore . . . lost to shame."[48]

But although Carpenter was sympathetic, crime historians like Luke Owen Pike, whose *History of Crime in England* was published between 1873 and 1876, felt that women who stayed home where they belonged would have no problems: "it follows that, [so] far as crime is determined by external circumstances, every step made by a woman towards her independence is a step towards that precipice at the bottom of which lies a prison."[49] Just in case anyone misunderstood, Pike went on to say that the more active and energetic women were, the more apt they were to end up as criminals. Nor was he the only one who thought so. Many Englishmen shared the view, anticipating the argument some criminologists advanced from a very different ideological perspective a century later, that when women achieved political and social equality, their crimes would resemble male crimes in both type and frequency.

But Carpenter understood women's potential very differently, stressing the contribution of ignorance and poverty to female criminality. In describing the convicted women she saw in the prisons as different from more privileged women actively seeking independence, she emphasized that their lower intellectual powers were the direct consequence of lack of education and cultivation.[50] She insisted that educated women from the upper classes were men's intellectual superiors when they were given equal opportunity to learn. Her clear implication is that disadvantaged women become involved in crime not from greed, immorality, or opportunity, but from *lack* of opportunity.

Nineteenth-century crime theorists also discussed the relationship between the economic situation in which women lived and the frequency with which they committed crime. Some of them, like the influential Italian criminologist Cesare Lombroso, felt that women were motived by greed: "women are more criminal in the more civilized countries. They are almost always drawn into crime by a false pride about their poverty, by a desire for luxury, and by masculine occupations and education, which give them the means and the opportunity to commit crimes."[51]

But in an opposing view the French criminologist Lambert Quetelet stressed that women in the higher classes were very rarely involved in crime, but that "descending into the lowest orders, the habits of both sexes resemble each other more and more."[52] His thesis asserts that education and economic condition had a greater impact on the prevalence of crime than gender or human nature, but his views had a mixed reception in England, in part because three distinct and conflicting perspectives on the nature of women's criminality were being advanced in Victorian social science. They all agreed that women committed crimes, especially serious crimes, much less frequently than men and explained that phenomenon, at least in part, by women's smaller size and lack of strength. But they agreed on little else.

The most clichéd approach, represented by Pike, Adam, and others like them, including Eliza Lynn Linton in some of her more acid moments, was that deviant women were evil—either temptresses who destroyed men through guile or gorgons who incapacitated them. Ignoring the petty criminality of the majority of culpable women and the domestic provocation which often explained one-time acts of violence, this informal school of misogynists found in the more spectacular criminal cases of the era plenty of evidence for their diatribes. The impact of their ideas on the public imagination was undeniably strong; the thesis that women were responsible for covert crime was frequently articulated and the image of the femme fatale dominated the graphic arts, especially at the century's end.

The most influential English theorists, like Herbert Spencer and Havelock Ellis, whose broad-ranging social analysis established their reputations in the emerging social sciences, believed that women were not by nature criminal. By emphasizing the biologically determined passivity of women, which they believed was universal and thus scarcely affected by social and political circumstances, they ignored poverty, abuse, and the lack of education and opportunity as influences which might provoke women to crime. Instead they blamed violence and aggression on sexual abnormality—by which they generally meant being too interested or experienced in sexual matters—or physical unattractiveness, as though being sexy or ugly were major motives for killing a husband or a baby.

The most insidious and persistent explanation, and the one which in various incarnations has been most controversial, assumed that women's criminality was the result of insanity provoked by menstruation, pregnancy, menopause, or other sex-related factors which were labeled dysfunctions because they were not masculine. In Susan Edwards's words, "badness" was redefined as "madness," and madness was the result of being a woman.[53] Although there was no reliable medical evidence to link normal biological experiences and insanity, the proponents of this explanation, W.W. Greg and Hugh Maudsley, for example, were convinced that a relationship existed and that it explained both sexual impropriety and criminality in women.

Despite a similar dearth of evidence to verify their conclusions, promulgators of the insanity school identified sexual impropriety as the genesis of biological problems (and the resulting insanity) in poor and working-class women while in more privileged (and moral) women, they concluded, biological factors drove them to insanity, immorality, and crime. The inconsistencies and the biases inherent in this explanation did little to deter its advocates or to impede its influence.

It is hardly surprising, given the conflicting explanations that were offered when women did not conform to either the expectation of superior morality or deeper depravity, that Victorian response to women's crimes was perplexed. Nor is it surprising that those crimes and their instigators became the subject of Victorian fiction.

THREE

Charles Dickens:
The Fiercest Impulses

Charles Dickens was an astute observer of a society where strife among intimates was often the norm. He built his fiction around the parents and children, husbands and wives, teachers and pupils, and partners in business who were embroiled in turmoil that frequently turned violent before it was resolved.[1] Half of that society were women, some of them victims of violence and others the perpetrators, and the novelist, with certain reluctance, included both kinds. While many—perhaps most—of his heroines seem insipid to the modern reader, his unconventional and sometimes physically violent women have a vitality the good women lack. Dickens described the potentially criminal women as rigidly restrained figures under intolerable duress, about to burst into uncontrollable fury, smashing everything in their path.[2] That image recurs throughout his novels, although his attitude toward such women became slightly but distinctly more tolerant. Each time he honed in on the same questions: when and why are women driven to violence, and does their violence mean they are less womanly?

His answer was that women can be criminalized by their environment, by marital abuse, and by oppression; in that candor he was ahead of his time. His murdering women, however, are foreign born or lower class or both. He never conceded that his middle-class countrywomen were capable of so explicit a threat to the status quo, perhaps because he refused to believe it himself or perhaps because he feared his audience's reaction. Equally conventionally, all of his women who even consider violence, as well as those who commit it, suffer an appropriate retribution. Yet despite these limitations, Dickens sets a precedent in Victorian fiction for creating credible deviant women.

In the early novels, young and poor women were victims either of physical abuse—for example, Nancy in *Oliver Twist* (1837)—or sexual exploitation—Little Em'ly and Rosa Dartle in *David Copperfield* (1850). In creating these characters, Dickens fictionalized and romanticized the girls he described in *Sketches By Boz*: the teenage prostitutes and petty thieves who end up as suicides if they do not die first of alcoholism, disease, or abuse.[3] Their own potential for violence, never far beneath the surface, is kept in check by the greater strength and determination of men who do not hesitate to coerce them into submission.[4]

Defined by class as well as gender, these women did not frighten or threaten middle-class readers. They picked pockets or worked as prostitutes, they went to jail at public expense, but they caused serious harm only to themselves and their intimates. Their underclass status is a critical component of Dickens's ability to make them sympathetic, and it also affirms the novelist's adherence to the Victorian truism that deviant women were different in kind from normal (that is, middle-class) women.

Nancy, in *Oliver Twist*, is his first criminal woman. Superficially she is a cliché: a Mary Magdelene, the sinner with a good soul. But Dickens is explicit, not only in the novel but in what he said about Nancy elsewhere, that her environment had been the genesis of her behavior, of what can be considered her criminality.[5] With that emphasis, he also negates two popular, but contradictory, contemporary explanations for criminality. In making the deprivations of her life so explicit, he undercuts the popular early Victorian assumption that criminals as a class were degenerate by choice.[6] In giving her no paternity, no last name, and making her no one's child, Dickens also makes it impossible to affirm that hers is inherited behavior. Nancy herself articulates why she is the way she is to the sympathetic

Rose Maylie: "Thank heaven upon your knees, dear lady, that you had friends to care for you and keep you in your childhood, *and that you were never in the midst of cold and hunger, and riot and drunkenness, and—and—something worse than all— as I have been from my cradle.* I may use the word, for the alley and the gutter were mine, as they will be my deathbed" (chap. 40, my italics). Dickens insists, particularly with the prissy but pointed allusion to sexual experience, that these handicaps are insurmountable for any woman who grows up the way Nancy has. For one thing, they put her too firmly under the control of strong men like Fagin and Sikes.

Although he might have anticipated the indignation it aroused in many readers, Dickens describes Nancy first as a bon vivant. She is at home in the criminal milieu, an associate of the master criminal Fagin (who is a pimp, a fence, a corrupter and abuser of children, a blackmailer, and a ruthless egotist); she trades her marginal independence as a prostitute for a kind of permanence as Bill Sikes's mistress. She drinks and swears (the mild expletives that Dickens lets his characters utter), lies and connives with no qualms. That boisterousness is essential to Dickens's conception of a thief's moll. For instance, when Fagin and Sikes want her to go to the police station to find out what has happened to Oliver, they have to coerce her with "threats, promises, and bribes." But having agreed, she rehearses the tears and moans for "her poor brother" with which she will regale the authorities, loving her role as entertainer and delighted that she can make Sikes laugh.

Despite this outward show of bravado, Nancy is enslaved by Sikes's power. For example, although Nancy laughs at his blunt rebuke when the robber scorns the impracticality of her avowed devotion, she turns pale and her hand trembles. Her pity for Oliver provokes her first confrontation with her lover and foreshadows her death. She implores the robber not to allow his vicious dog to attack the boy: "I don't care for that, Bill, I don't care for that. . . . the child shan't be torn down by the dog, *unless you kill me first*" (chap. 16, my italics). She defies Fagin too, grabs the stick he threatens Oliver with, and throws it in the fire. For the first time, Dickens raises the specter of a

No scene in Victorian fiction evokes the outrage of domestic violence more powerfully than F.W. Pailthorpe's depiction of Bill Sykes beating the defenseless Nancy to death.

woman out of control, as his narrator comments: "There is something about a roused woman: especially if she adds to all her other strong passions, the fiercest impulses of recklessness and despair: which few men like to provoke" (chap. 16).

Having gone that far, Dickens reneges on the possibility that Nancy can use her rage to make positive changes in her own life. True, she is able to help Oliver by alerting his friends to the danger he is in. But when it comes to helping herself either by leaving her ghetto or by getting rid of Bill (even Fagin thinks she should poison the abusive robber), she lacks the will to act. Modern readers recognize what is now identified as the battered-woman syndrome in Nancy's behavior.

Nancy's joie de vivre disappears as she begins to understand her hopeless position. Oliver's naive impressions of her beauty and jollity are contrasted later in the novel with descriptions of her being "so pale and reduced with watching and privation, that there would have been considerable difficulty in recognizing her" (chap. 39). Nancy's anxiety about Oliver, her hatred of Fagin, and her suffering from Bill Sikes's constant abuse age her beyond her seventeen years. And while she still uses her "feminine charm" to cope with Sikes, she has little energy for the violent hysterics or infectious clowning of just a few months before.

In the final analysis, Dickens does not resolve—and readers cannot agree on—why Nancy sticks it out with Sikes. Is she a truer woman because she stays by her man? Is she pathetic because as a battered woman she is unable to sever the abusive relationship? Is she so limited by her background that she cannot comprehend a "marriage" without physical violence? Or is she right that, had she left him or killed him, there would be no place for her in the rigidly moral Victorian society?

The answer to each question is yes. Dickens is concerned with Nancy's status as a woman because a basic assumption of Victorian society was that womanly women did not commit crimes. Nancy herself thinks she has little womanhood left because her sensibilities have been eroded to the point that crime and criminals are tolerable to her. The narrator seems to agree, pointing out her brazen aggressiveness in venturing out of her own community and her strident insistence on meeting Rose Maylie face to face. His definition of womanliness means modesty, purity, and diffidence, and he expects lower-class women to know their place.

But the novel actually emphasizes the opposite view, refuting the idea that women who take the law into their own hands are by definition unwomanly. Nancy's physical victimization bonds her to other women, including middle-class women, who are abused by their husbands, lovers, or fathers. Dickens's description of Sikes beating her to death initiated the era's reluctant recognition that inhumane treatment rather than the lack of womanliness was an important cause of criminality. Nancy also suffers psychologically for her guilt in ways that her male companions do not. They relish their criminal careers while she is resigned to hers; they have no compunction about destroying a child or killing a woman; nor are they in any way sympathetic, although Dickens makes a flimsy effort in each case to suggest that some humanity is buried in their psyches. Perhaps most important, for Dickens, is that Nancy knows middle-class life is better than what she has; Fagin and Sikes do not.

Nancy is most conventionally womanly in her inability to make things happen by herself. Despite her crucial part in resolving the threat to Oliver, she depends on Mr. Brownlow to take action. Here, as in her decision to return to Sikes, she is ineffective by herself. She needs the authority of men to validate what her instincts tell her is right. Her impotence and her ultimate defeat make her—and women like her—sympathetic because they pose no threat to the status quo or to the dominance of men.

Paul Squires may be right that such a girl would never, in reality, have befriended Oliver or betrayed Fagin.[7] But it is also true that Nancy is "the only one of [Dickens's] early female characters that can be taken seriously," in large part because Dickens was obsessed with understanding her.[8] If Nancy is not true to life, she is true to Dickens's conviction that even the most appalling circumstances would not erase innate womanliness. Nevertheless, he makes clear from the start that women who violate the rigid decorum of society have no chance of survival, however generous their feelings or profound their suffering. He was not yet ready to create a woman hard enough and self-reliant enough to defy that convention. But in seeing Nancy's ultimate fate as catastrophe rather than retribution, he leaves the subject of women's criminal behavior open to development.

Ironically, despite Nancy's undeniable sexuality, it was not Dickens but his contemporary and rival William Makepeace Thackeray who made women criminals' sexuality an explicit component of Victorian fiction. Outraged at Dickens's sentimental treatment of Nancy, Thackeray based his satirical novel *Catherine* (1839) on the actual case of Catherine Hayes, who was burned at the stake in 1725 for convincing her son and a lodger to kill her husband. Although he justified the novel's exaggerated and graphic details of a hatchet murder followed by decapitation as an attempt to arrest the offensive practice of arousing sympathy for immoral women, Thackeray described a highly sexed woman who planned the murder so she could marry her lover. Beth Kalikoff believes that the novelist failed in his determination to make Catherine repulsive, and that she is, instead, a rather "engaging character."[9] She may even be the unwitting prototype of some of sensation fiction's more assertive heroines. In any case, because Catherine's motive was grounded so firmly in her licentiousness, Thackeray opened the way for much more explicit correlation of sexuality and criminality in later Victorian fiction.

Abusive men who goad women to reckless behavior and violence appear throughout the Dickens canon. After Nancy's brutal murder, no other woman was beaten to death, in part because the dramatic intensity of that scene would have been impossible to replicate and in part because the predominantly middle-class abusers in his other novels were permitted more subtle (though equally destructive) methods of asserting their will. But as men like Mr. Murdstone and Bentley Drummle assault children and animals, Dickens's decision not to describe them hitting their wives panders to the fiction of middle-class respectability and restraint. He leaves no doubt, though, that strong women grow bitter and age before their time while weaker ones die as the result of abusive marriages.

In *Dombey and Son* (1848), Edith Dombey is subjected to an intolerable marital relationship because she will not subjugate herself totally to her husband. Arrogant and vengeful, he orders her to behave as he demands without regard for her legitimate objections or her candid effort to assess the difficulties between them (chap. 10). When, through Carker, his self-serving clerk, Dombey threatens harm to his much-despised daughter if Edith continues to befriend the girl, he has driven Edith to become a destroyer. Modeling her revenge on his technique of psychological torture, she chooses to disgrace him by dramatically eloping with Carker rather than murdering him outright. The shame of an unfaithful wife is compounded by financial ruin linked to the elopement, and Dombey is never the same again.

Bowing to convention, Dickens tried to soften the implicit message in the situation he had created, that a woman is justified in striking back at abusive marital behavior. Edith is unsatisfied despite her revenge, though she never questions the validity of her decision to run away. Dombey is awakened to his failure as a human being and rescued from a bitter and lonely life by the redeeming love of his forgiving daughter and her family. But no attentive reader can miss the connection between abuse and its destructive consequences. Without Edith Dombey's revenge, Dombey would never have accepted Florence; the girl's suffering is efficacious only because her father is totally emasculated by his loss of face and fortune.

The most dramatic scene, the one with the clearest subtext about a woman's conflicted determination and reluctance to murder, takes place when the eloping couple rendezvous. When Carker wants to claim his privileges as lover, Edith holds him off with a knife and threatens to kill him. There is no question in the clerk's mind, or in the reader's, that she would do it. In part she is protecting the honor she holds dear despite the public assumption of her sin. In part she is asserting her social and moral superiority over an inferior man. But the real point is made in Carker's insolent inquiry, "Do you mistake me for your husband?" and the disdain in her refusal to answer him (chap. 24). Destroying Dombey was exhilarating; killing this second and in some ways more repulsive "husband" would be equally so. Although Edith does not directly cause Carker's gruesome death when she warns him he is being pursued, the powerful train that mutilates his body is surely an allusion to the metaphor we have already noted—the roused woman as destructive force—and his death is just as surely a consequence of his chauvinistic assumption that he could manipulate Edith Dombey for his own convenience.[10]

In the Dombey women's differing responses to abuse, Dickens

"Phiz" (Hablot K. Browne) demonstrates that Mr. Carker is wrong in this scene from *Dombey and Son*. The triumph is not Carker's but Edith Dombey's as she repels his advances and sends him inadvertently to his death. But, like most strong women, she is shown as arrogant and unwomanly.

revives the debate about appropriate womanly behavior to suggest that Florence in craving her father's love is truer to nature.
Yet he has made Edith's motives for vengeance too powerful to
erase with a happy reunion or negate with her own suffering
or death. Thus to conclude, as Louise Yellin does, that the
novel's final message is that "submission succeeds where rebellion fails," is to ignore the reality that without Edith's rebellion,
Florence's submission was powerless.[11] Inexorably, if perhaps
unwillingly, Dickens was moving toward a more innovative view
of the violent woman.

It is a theme he returns to in *Bleak House* (1853). The central
point of its murder story is that the lawyer Tulkinghorn is a
bully, sadistically delighted with the torture he can inflict on
Lady Dedlock, a woman of power and determination, when he
uncovers an illicit love affair in her carefully hidden past. He
confronts her with the evidence he has ferreted out, not to
blackmail her but to destroy her social position and her marriage.
All he offers, if she plays the game his way and lets him call all
the shots, is an effort to keep the news of her shame from wide
distribution. His determination to ruin her seems to defy logic;
there is nothing for him to gain except the hollow self-satisfaction
of upholding the morality of the upper-class he serves. But
Tulkinghorn is an inadequate man threatened by a strong and
beautiful woman in a society where strong women are abhorred.

The sexual politics of their encounter provides an undercur-
rent of tension which Dickens does not fully elaborate but which
is crucial to the intensity of their struggle. Lady Dedlock does
not concede easily, and he nearly falters before her enormous
self-control. Beneath her assertive demeanor, he senses the
anger which drives her reaction to him despite the fear and
shame which burden her. But he underestimates the degree to
which he is vulnerable.

On the very night he announces that her time is up, Tulkinghorn is shot through the heart. The narrator titillates us.
Lady Dedlock is out walking at the fatal moment in a state of
high anxiety: "Her soul is turbulent within her; she is sick at
heart, and restless. The large rooms are too cramped. . . . Too
capricious and imperious in all she does, to be the cause of much

surprise in those about her as to anything she does, this woman loosely muffled, goes out into the moonlight" (chap. 49).

In the grip of suspicion and circumstantial evidence, she agonizes: "Her enemy he was and she has often, often, often wished him dead. Her enemy he is, even in his grave. This dreadful accusation comes upon her, like a new torment at his lifeless hand. And when she recalls how she was secretly at his door that night, . . . she shudders as if the hangman's hands were at her neck. . . . The horror that is upon her, is unutterable" (chap. 55). Lady Dedlock does not kill him because he is already dead when she reaches him. But her intent and the realization of that intent shock and depress her. She resolves to die herself, not only for the "wicked relief she felt at Tulkinghorn's death" but in retribution for her guilty past. Once the truth has been discovered—her capacity for passionate love and violent murder made known—she can no longer maintain the arrogance which sustains her.

But if she does not kill Tulkinghorn, who does? Lady Dedlock's maid, Mademoiselle Hortense, is a much more credible killer to Dickens's readers than Lady Dedlock—even with her questionable morals. Hortense's willingness to cooperate with Tulkinghorn in uncovering the evidence to discredit Lady Dedlock reveals her disrespect for her betters. And her image as a "she-Wolf imperfectly tamed" (chap. 12) raises the specter of an unwomanly woman. Given the fact that she is female, lower class, and foreign born, Dickens needed little else to demonstrate her capacity for violence, especially because of his implicit allusions to the case of Maria Manning, a one-time lady's maid who had been executed in 1849 for shooting a discarded lover.[12]

There is, between Hortense and Tulkinghorn, as well as between Tulkinghorn and Lady Dedlock, a gender-based tension. Despite Hortense's help in his crusade against Lady Dedlock, the lawyer feels no reciprocal obligation to make good on his promises of reward. She is not worth his trouble. In this sense, Tulkinghorn invites his own death, for Hortense is no dupe to be manipulated, no victim to be threatened. He attempts in their final, fatal interview to rid himself of the aggravation of her importunate demands by reminding her that her mistress has called her "implacable and unmanageable," and suggesting that she is not worthy of another job. But Hortense lacks the Lady's self-control and guilty conscience, lacks the Lady's dread of disgrace, but most of all lacks social deference. When Tulkinghorn threatens her, she threatens back:

> "And now," proceeds the lawyer, still without minding her, "you had better go. Think twice before you come here again."
> "Think you," she answers, "twice two hundred times." [chap. 42]

None of the fierceness which drives Hortense to kill Tulkinghorn, or the cunning to act as if she were shocked at his death, or the calculated meanness with which she tries to incriminate Lady Dedlock can protect her from being found out. When Bucket arrests her, she calls him "pig" and "devil" and "liar," but she puts up little resistance and seems to take pride in the fact that Tulkinghorn is dead and Lady Dedlock is shamed. She is just as firm and resolute in her captivity, unafraid of anyone. Of her likely execution Dickens has nothing to say, as he shifts the focus to resolve the larger themes of the novel.[13]

Dickens has done a perplexing thing, though, in suggesting that two women are guilty of Tulkinghorn's murder, especially as they have a similar motive in his arrogant misogyny. There can be no question that the novelist understands the genesis of women's violence, especially when it is fomented by the abusive behavior of men. He leaves little doubt that Lady Dedlock could have killed Tulkinghorn, just as Edith Dombey would have killed Carker. But Dickens never does risk having a woman who is sympathetic by virtue of class and ethnicity guilty of literal violence; he is too much of his time to concede the possibility although he describes very persuasive motives.

Here, as in *Dombey and Son*, a wronged woman focuses reader attention on gender conflict and its potential consequences. Dickens describes women with an overriding determination to act: not to be feminine and dependent but to be assertive and aggressive. Again, too, he contrasts those strong women with mild ones who do not struggle but accept their proper place. But Esther Summerson in this novel, like Florence Dombey earlier, makes much less impact on the modern reader's sense of what it meant to be a Victorian woman than either Lady Dedlock or Mademoiselle Hortense.

In *Great Expectations* (1861), a later and less sanguine book, Dickens reworks his ideas about the violent potential of impoverished women in his sketch of Molly, the "wild beast tamed," whose acquittal of murder was engineered by the lawyer Jaggers in spite of her guilt. The new twist is that Molly has committed a particularly violent crime, the strangulation of another woman. Yet Molly, despite her strength, is at the mercy of a man more powerful than she. That man is not her lover, whose infidelities provoked her crime, but Jaggers himself. His control over her is not physical; he never raises his hand or his voice. Rather, he "holds her [always] in suspense" (chap. 26), as he knows not only her guilt but the whereabouts of the child he has forced her to relinquish as a condition of defending her.[14]

Jaggers believes that a vengeful woman must be controlled by being repeatedly humiliated, a task Molly's status as his domestic servant makes easy. Indeed, he considers it a mark of his manhood that he has bent her to his will. The fact that he feels no similar compunction to control Magwitch or any other murdering man proves that he thinks violent women a much greater threat to society (even when their victims are other women) than men. Nor does he consider that Molly's twenty-year-old crime has been expiated. Dickens does not explain why a defense attorney who has defended the worst of criminals thinks that way. Nor does he have Pip or Wemmick make any objection when Jaggers tells them about "asserting his power over her in the old way" (chap. 51). The novelist is a realist when he describes women's potential for violence, but he is still bound by the convention that a woman who acts on that potential is anathema.

In *A Tale of Two Cities* (1859) Dickens describes a woman whose criminal milieu is public rather than domestic and whose violent tendencies are unrestrained by the conventional, feminine conscience that holds his English women in check. Cold-hearted, unemotional, and unforgiving, she is a prototype of the unwomanly woman later nineteeth-century criminologists condemned as more incorrigible than men, and an adumbration of the modern specter, the terrorist. Madame DeFarge does not seem so bloody-minded when Dickens introduces her. A good businesswoman with an adoring husband, she enjoys the marital security that the novelist's other women so frequently yearn for and so rarely find. Her chief avocation is knitting, a quiet domestic task; only later does the reader discover that DeFarge's needles produce neither shawls nor baby clothes but a deathlist of her enemies and the enemies of the French Revolution.

Like Dickens's other women criminals, DeFarge has a motive. The individual revenge she craves has a basis in personal experience. Her lovely elder sister has been ravaged and destroyed by the aristocratic Evremondes, and her young brother killed in trying to avenge her. She is implacable in her determination to destroy the remaining member of that family, known as Charles Darnay. Of her more general hatred of the old regime, she says that she has seen so much suffering by "sister-women" that she is immune to isolated instances or unhappy individuals (bk. 3, chap. 3). The combination of her personal rage and revolutionary passion has destroyed whatever compassion and tenderness she may have once had but which the nineteenth-century reader expected in a woman.

The French Revolution provided Dickens with the perfect setting.[15] One great appeal was that it offered a model for a murderous woman who was not English. Surely the labor unrest in the Midlands mill towns could have provided an environment to spawn a woman who was violent for ideological as well as personal reasons, but it was an option Dickens did not use. Dickens conceived of DeFarge as both a mother and a child of 1789; her fury is the fury of the people who brought the revolution to life, and her violence is the product of that turmoil which she helped to create. To convey her empowered but ultimately self-destructive womanhood, he looks at her from three perspectives: in relation to her co-conspirators and accomplices in the Revolution, her personal enemies, and her husband.

Madame DeFarge is a venerated leader of the Revolution. Armed with an axe, a loaded pistol, and a dagger (distinctly unwomanly and undeniably phallic weapons), she joins the attack on the Bastille at the head of an army of women, urged on by her chief lieutenant, a woman called The Vengeance. DeFarge insists that women can kill as well as men, especially women armed with "hunger and revenge." She herself cuts off the head of the slaughtered governor of the Bastille, a revolutionary Judith bloodying her shoe as she steadies the corpse to mutilate it. Knitting has given way to slaughter, yet DeFarge's demeanor is as controlled and determined as it is in the domestic scenes which precede it.

The narrator notes that the men in their revolutionary fervor and desire for vengeance are awful to look at, "but the women were a sight to chill the boldest" (bk. 2, chap. 22). The admiration her leadership garners for DeFarge knows no bounds. When she expresses dismay at her husband's compassion, her fellow revolutionaries call her "adorable" and "my cherished." She is also admired, ironically, for her "fine figure, and her superb moral endowments"—the astounding combination of these most feminine of epithets applied to the most unfeminine of women intensifies the complexity of Dickens's characterization (bk. 3, chap. 14).

The passion of her revolutionary beliefs and her devotion to the memory of her destroyed family make Therese DeFarge implacable about her personal enemies: Charles Darnay, his wife Lucie, and even Lucie's long-suffering father, Dr. Manette. Likening her own urgency for revenge to the force of wind and fire, DeFarge is unmoved by Lucie's gentleness or the knowledge that it was Manette who treated her dying sister and brother and fruitlessly denounced the Evremondes to the monarchy. Her plan is to provoke Lucie into condemning the Republic in the moments following Darnay's execution; then Lucie can be denounced and destroyed, too. Her insatiable vengeance distills the essence of her character even more clearly than her perverse pleasure at watching executions.[16]

Therese DeFarge's relationship with her husband is a curious and malleable one. As the novel begins, they seem well suited and mutually admiring. She is his business partner, his ally in radical politics, his confidante. Of the two, she is more certain that the people's revenge is at hand, but she encourages his zeal rather than demeaning his hesitancy. He thinks of her as "a real woman, a strong woman, a grand woman, a frightfully grand woman" (bk. 2, chap. 16) and urges his customers to "confide in Madame DeFarge" (bk. 2, chap. 15). They disagree, though, about the Manettes; he insists the blood-letting must stop somewhere, a conclusion based in reason and moderation alien to his wife. She is not mollified, and proceeds without him—a daring, aggressive, unwomanly course of action.

In contrast to the nineteenth-century axiom that a criminal woman was a dupe or agent of a strong man, we see in Madame DeFarge a de facto "strong man," a woman who will sacrifice anything, including her marriage or her own life, to accomplish her goals. A clear sense of her unique place in Dickens's fiction is found at the end of the novel:

> There were many women at that time, upon whom the time laid a dreadfully disfiguring hand; but, there was not one among them more to be dreaded than this ruthless woman. . . . Of a strong and fearless character, of shrewd sense and readiness, of great determination, of that kind of beauty which not only seems to impart to its possessor firmness and animosity, but to strike into others an instinctive recognition of those qualities; the troubled times would have heaved her up, under any circumstances. But, imbued from her childhood with a brooding sense of wrong, and an inveterate hatred of a class, opportunity had developed her into a tigress. She was absolutely without pity. If she had ever had the virtue in her, it had quite gone out of her. [bk. 3, chap. 14]

DeFarge is killed when her own gun is knocked askew in a struggle with Lucie's devoted servant, Miss Pross. Because DeFarge has been introduced as the woman who never makes mistakes, her final error, underestimating the intensity of

Pross's affection and her willingness to risk herself in defense of those she loves, is even more ironic and bitter.

As bold as Dickens is in writing about violent women, he is bound by the conventions of his age and his own prejudices. He gives women motives for murder but in the early novels stops short of physical violence and literal guilt. Instead, he punished their abusers himself; it is no coincidence that Sikes and Fagin, Dombey and Carker, and Tulkinghorn are destroyed and die. Later, Hortense and Therese DeFarge, "wicked foreign women," and the gypsy Mollie do kill, but for the novelist they are inferior women.[17]

Sexual tension, everywhere implicit in the actions of the abused women, is not made an explicit component of their aggression. In this, the novelist avoids antagonizing an audience that was not yet used to the possibility that a normal English-woman's passions—intense love or hate—could drive her to act violently. Thus Dickens counterbalances his increasing realism in acknowledging women's capacity for certain kinds of crime with a persistent sense that such criminality cannot be allowed if society is to function. But the undercurrents of gender-based tension as a motive and even a justification of violence set the course that Victorian fiction followed.

FOUR

George Eliot: My Heart Said, "Die!"

Women who consider violent solutions to their misery and despair appear throughout George Eliot's fiction from *Scenes of Clerical Life* (1858) to *Daniel Deronda* (1876). Nearly all are English, representing all social classes. The warring urges within them are resolved only when they sublimate their rage and sacrifice themselves for another's (usually a man's) well-being, adhering to the Christian, Victorian model of acceptable womanly behavior. Those women incapable of self-denial follow a more troubled path, pitching themselves and their domestic environments into turmoil. But it would be a mistake to think, based on this pattern, that Eliot's treatment of women is conventional or repressive. By emphasizing the desperation and the agony that women experience before they commit a violent act, the novelist shows how natural, how womanly, the need is to protect themselves and their self-esteem. In so doing she creates a new awareness of violence done in the name of self-preservation.

Caterina Sarti, a character from "Mr. Gilfil's Love Story," the second tale in *Scenes of Clerical Life*, begins by passionately loving her guardian's nephew, Captain Anthony Wybrow, and ends by hating him enough to murder him. Though he is indifferent to her adoration, she feels and behaves like a seduced, abandoned, and maligned woman; it is her sense of being abused that precipitates her rage and her plan to stab him.

Eliot hints at Caterina's potential for violence from the earliest scenes, dwelling on her "fierceness." Although she is little, even bird-like, her nature is one of "intense love and fierce jealousy" that resists all authoritarian discipline. "The only thing in which Caterina showed any precocity was a certain ingenuity in vindictiveness" (chap. 4). When she realizes Wybrow is promoting her marriage to Mr. Gilfil to distract her attention from himself, Caterina's misery becomes such a "mad passion" that she hurls her beloved's picture across the room, stopping just short of grinding the pieces into the floor. The narrator bursts out: "God send [that such] relenting may always come before the worst irrevocable deed" (chap. 12). That entreaty becomes a primary theme in Eliot's treatment of enraged women.

Later on, Caterina's rage shows no such restraint. Not only has Wybrow betrayed her love by agreeing to marry a rich, eligible woman, but he has also betrayed her confidence to his fiancée. The girl's violent frenzy is made quite explicit: "See how she rushes noiselessly, like a pale meteor, along the passages and up the gallery stairs! Those gleaming eyes, those bloodless lips, that swift silent tread, make her look like the incarnation of a fierce purpose, rather than a woman. . . . Yes, there are sharp weapons in the gallery. There is a dagger in that cabinet; she knows it well. . . . she darts into the cabinet, takes out the dagger, and thrusts it into her pocket. . . . He will be there— he will be before her in a moment. He will come toward her with that false smile, thinking she does not know his baseness— *she will plunge the dagger into his heart*" (chap. 13, my italics). Caterina never gets her chance; providence intervenes. Within minutes, Wybrow is dead of a heart attack.[1]

Caterina's guilt is profound. She believes that she can never be forgiven because she intended to kill. Mr. Gilfil, the clergyman who loves her, tries to persuade her that she is not alone in her will to do evil. He insists, perhaps correctly, that had she really had the opportunity to kill she would not have carried it out. In reminding her of Wybrow's provocation, Gilfil suggests that some women are driven to violent action in response to abuse— a reaction that modern criminologists label victim-precipitated crime.[2] "Wrong makes wrong," Gilfil admonishes. "When people use us ill, we can hardly help having ill feelings towards them, but that second wrong is more excusable" (chap. 19).

Eliot hesitates here, as she does in the novels that follow, to carry the implications of this justification for retaliation to their logical conclusion. But the comment is a pregnant one, because it recognizes a woman's need for revenge as explicable and natural.

Caterina Sarti's misery is self-indulgent: she imagines herself abused by a lover who never thought about her as a sexual or marital partner and who intended her no harm. Janet Dempster's is not. The alcoholic and abused wife in "Janet's Repentence," the final story in *Scenes of Clerical Life*, lives a tortured existence. Her husband batters her physically and psychologically through fifteen years of a disastrous marriage. Everyone in the community knows she is abused, but nobody intervenes, in part because Janet pretends that nothing is wrong. Eliot clearly blames Dempster, not Janet, for the situation. An abusive person requires opportunity, not motive, the novelist's conventional male narrator insists. Furthermore, Janet's need to resist, or to strike back, is vitiated by the insidious effects of alcoholism which undermines her self-confidence as it feeds her husband's need to brutalize her. Her greatest dread is leaving or being forced to leave. "Better this misery," she thinks, "than the blank that lay . . . outside her married home" (chap. 13). Eliot has fastened, more explicitly than Dickens, on what held Victorian women in abusive marriages. There was nowhere to go.[3]

Janet's wild swings of emotion, from assertive resolution to depression, finally come to a head when Dempster rejects one last gesture of conciliation and she refuses, at long last, to hide the discord from their guests. But rather than leaving him, she goes to bed convinced that he is going to kill her. Her fleeting defiance is replaced by terror when he thrusts her, dressed only in a nightgown, out into the cold night.

Again Eliot backs away from confrontation; Janet feels "too crushed, too faulty, too liable to reproach, to have the courage, even if she had the wish" to seek public redress (chap. 16) or private vengeance. Instead this battered alcoholic becomes an

Evangelical saint who resolves, on her clergyman's misguided advice, to go back to Dempster to try again. But while Eliot seems to advocate conciliation, she provides poetic justice: within twenty-four hours of throwing her out of the house, Dempster lies dying from a drunken-driving accident.

Before his death, Dempster hallucinates, imagining Janet as mythic monster, her black hair turned to snakes: " 'Let me go, let me go,' he said in a loud, hoarse whisper; 'she's coming . . . she's cold . . . she's dead . . . she'll strangle me with her black hair. 'Ah!' he shrieked aloud, 'her hair is all serpents . . . they're black serpents . . . they hiss . . . they hiss . . . let me go . . . she wants to drag me with her cold arms . . . her arms are serpents . . . they are great white serpents . . . they'll twine around me . . . she wants to drag me into the cold water . . . her bosom is cold . . . it is black . . . it is all serpents' " (chap. 23). There is no clearer literary example of the Victorian man's obsession with woman as predatory demon, an obsession that Nina Auerbach has clearly elaborated in *The Woman and the Demon* and Bram Dijkstra has comprehensively illustrated in *Idols of Perversity.*[4] But Janet is no predator; she is a victim who is incapable of reacting violently to abuse despite what her abuser expects as his just reward.

Eliot's publisher, Blackwood, objected to the "commonality" of the Dempsters' marriage, but the novelist insisted that she had "softened" the details of the real marriage she used as her source. She even threatened to withdraw the story if the magazine would not publish it as written.[5] When Blackwood acquiesced, she reaffirmed her eagerness to continue to write for him, explaining that she wanted her work to "stir men's hearts to sympathy." "My artistic bent is not at all to the presentation of eminently irreproachable characters, but to the presentation of mixed human beings in such a way as to call forth tolerant judgment, pity, and sympathy."[6]

Stirring sympathy for Hetty Sorrel, whose child-murder is the focus of the most dramatic episodes in Eliot's first novel, *Adam Bede* (1859), was one of the novelist's reasons for choosing so timely and so controversial a subject.

No crime a woman commits is more dramatic than infanticide,

and none evokes more complex or more contradictory responses. No author had ever completely resolved how an audience ought to react to a mother's act of violence against her own children. At the climax of Euripides' *Medea* one is torn between pity for the woman's agony and revulsion at the murder of her sons, appalled and relieved when she is whisked away from her inevitable punishment by a deus ex machina. In Defoe's *Roxana* the title character's daughter's obnoxious and pointless persistence in exposing Roxana's identity almost justifies the girl's disappearance. But there is a significant difference between Medea's vengeful action, the maid Amy's defense of her mistress, and the motives for infanticide in Eliot's novel. Medea's children were not babies, and the shame of illegitimate birth did not create moral and emotional turmoil or precipitate her violence. Roxana's daughter gambles on extortion and loses. Shame and dread of the misery that shame would bring explain Hetty Sorrel's treatment of her child.

In addition to Wordsworth's "The Thorn" and Sir Walter Scott's *The Heart of Midlothian*, the literary sources she acknowledged, Eliot knew at least one true story like Hetty's because her aunt, Elizabeth Evans, a traveling Methodist preacher, served as confessor and companion to a convicted child murderer, Mary Voce, who was executed in Nottingham in March 1802.[7] She knew, too, that infanticide was as a serious contemporary problem as spouse abuse was. In 1856 the Reverend William Smith, fired with moral indignation, wrote an outraged article for the *Saturday Review*, reporting that mothers accused of infanticide were being regularly acquitted in the courts.[8] Calling Medea more justified in her actions than the girls whom "juries will not convict," Smith insisted that this leniency gave tacit approval to the crimes and encouraged promiscuity.

Smith was right that the acquittals in infanticide cases that got as far as the courts were disproportionate to adjudications in other capital cases, despite the increasingly sophisticated means for determining the cause and timing of infants' deaths. But some of Smith's contemporaries, including Eliot, rejected his assumption that eroding moral standards were behind the acquittals and that behavior could be changed by more frequent guilty verdicts and executions. To capture the intensity of sentiment against girls like Hetty, Eliot put Smith's opinions into the vehement reaction of the otherwise generous and kind schoolteacher, Bartle Massey, when he hears the news of Hetty's arrest: "I think the sooner such women are put out o' the world the better: and the men that help 'em to do mischief had better go along with 'em for that matter. What good will you do by keeping such vermin alive? eating the victual that 'ud feed rational beings" (Chap. 40). Massey, like Smith and many of his countrymen, was unable or unwilling to fathom that infanticide was not only the wrenching culmination of one girl's physical and emotional desperation but also the larger fault of a rigid and false morality.[9]

The more insightful citizens, obviously including many jurors, distinguished between the middle-class repugnance at premarital sex and working-class culture where women were frequently pregnant before marriage, especially in agricultural communities where proof of fertility was traditional and important.[10] Since the majority of infanticide defendants were—like Hetty—single, working-class women who had been abandoned by men, juries saw them as victims rather than criminals. There also seems to have been an increasing willingness to accept temporary insanity or physical debility following birth as exculpatory defenses, especially in cases when the births were unattended.

To link her controversial heroine to these tragic defendants rather than to the culpable child-murdering figure of the apocryphal Lilith, Eliot's novel is full of premonitions of Hetty's inadvertent disaster. Before her brief affair with Arthur Donnithorne and the resulting pregnancy, Hetty is sexually innocent—a charming, vulnerable seventeen-year-old. But, as Eliot warns, "[hers] was a springtide beauty, round-limbed, gambolling, circumventing you by a false air of innocence—the innocence of a star-browed calf, for example, that *being inclined for a promenade out of bounds, leads you . . . to a stand in the middle of a bog*" (chap. 7, my italics). Hetty is interested in Arthur Donnithorne because she thinks he will provide an escape from the unexciting existence of the family's dairy and the prospect of a dull marriage and its inevitable children. This is the first intimation of "hardness," the lack of conventional womanliness, that ultimately works so much against her when she expresses no maternal anguish about her dead infant. By a curious double standard, often a defendant's inconsolable sorrow for her dead child was a major factor in winning an acquittal in infanticide cases.

The misery in store for Hetty is foreshadowed long before she runs away from home, terrified and despairing, to avoid her impending marriage to Adam Bede and certain discovery of her pregnancy. When Arthur returns to his regiment, he fears she might "do something violent in her grief" (chap. 29). The narrator sounds an even more ominous note: "Hers was a luxurious and vain nature, not a passionate one; and if she were ever to take any *violent measure*, she must be urged to it by the *desperation of terror*" (chap. 31, my italics). Torn between her urgency to live and her dread of shame and disgrace, Hetty cannot commit suicide and she will not risk discovery. Eliot, who evokes great pity for Hetty, although she never infuses her with the appeal of her later, more intelligent heroines, insists that the girl's "narrow heart and narrow thoughts" had "no room . . . for any sorrows but her own" (chap. 37). After her baby's premature birth, she resumes her encumbered journey through the wooded countryside with nowhere to go and no apparent recourse.

There she commits a mindless act with violent consequences: she abandons the baby by hiding it in a hollow in the ground and covering it with branches, telling herself that someone may find it and take care of it. Clearly, reason plays no part in this act, nor malice, nor premeditation. She intends the baby no direct harm, but she cannot deceive herself for very long that everything will be all right. When she returns to the baby's hiding place, she is arrested for murder.[11]

The climax of the novel, the contrast between the harsh judgment in the male-dominated courtroom and the compassion and forgiveness her cousin Dinah offers in the prison cell, emphasizes Eliot's understanding of child-murder. The jury's hasty guilty verdict is based on Hetty's obstinacy in denying guilt. For the jury, "the unnaturalness of her crime stood out more harshly by the side of her hard immovability and obstinate silence" (chap. 43). But Eliot's point is that the crime is not unnatural; rather, it is the all too natural consequence of Hetty's personality in the context of her environment.

Extenuating circumstances make the judgment unjust, although Hetty is unquestionably guilty of the negligent death of the baby. Post-partum depression and physical exhaustion were not considered as mitigating factors; neither was her lack of premeditation. Furthermore, Hetty was absolutely right that she and her baby had nowhere to go, but she lacked the self-discipline and the intellectual distance which help Eliot's middle-class women resist violent responses to those people and circumstances which put them at jeopardy.[12]

In examining how Hetty's very ordinary life came to such disaster, Eliot is forthright about what drives this woman to violence. Hetty's crime, to the extent that she is responsible for what she does, is the result of self-absorption, her self-devoted rather than her self-devoting love. And while those traits are not admirable, they are neither immoral nor unnatural. When Hetty finally admits the details of her experience to her cousin Dinah, Dinah's (and Eliot's) compassionate view that the baby's murder is explicable in human terms and that the perpetrator ought to be the object of pity is a daring one, not equalled in serious Victorian fiction until Hardy's *Tess of the D'Urbervilles*. Unlike Tess, though, Hetty is saved from hanging by a last-minute reprieve secured by Arthur Donnithorne—a melodramatic but powerful moment.[13]

In having Hetty die during her passage back to England after serving her seven-year sentence, Eliot rules out the possibility of a romantic reunion with Donnithorne. Joan Mannheimer suggests that Eliot shies away from the implicit message of the novel—that a radical transformation of the social structure was possible—because that change meant acknowledging Hetty's sexuality, something Eliot avoided despite the sexual intercourse that led to her catastrophe. In Mannheimer's words, Hetty "violates the absolute barrier between domesticity and sexuality essential to the Victorian mythology surrounding wife and

Hetty turns away from the dreadful spectre of the gallows in J. Jellicoe's illustration for *Adam Bede*. So does George Eliot, preventing the execution with an eleventh-hour reprieve. Hetty's death, though not a violent one, is still inevitable.

mother," a barrier Eliot was not ready to assault.[14] It seems to me equally plausible that Eliot is too realistic to transform Hetty, despite her suffering, into anybody's happy wife. But whatever her reason for killing off Hetty before she can return to Donnithorne, Eliot also rejects the conventional Victorian perception that illicit sexuality caused a woman's criminality: Hetty's premarital sexual experience is not the reason she kills her baby. Ignorance and isolation are.

Eliot did not again create a character like Hetty or more than one Bertha Latimer ("The Lifted Veil," 1859), whose plot to poison her strange husband is foiled by a combination of clairvoyance and hocus-pocus. Instead Eliot's women respond to oppressive, abusive, or otherwise intolerable husbands in a series of novels where, as Judith Wilt points out, marriage itself is repeatedly conceived of as murder. For example, in *Middlemarch* (1872) Dorothea Brooke Casaubon, the heroine, feels enormous rage against her ineffectual and vindictive husband, but her anger and its potentially destructive consequences are kept under control by her strength of will: "The energy that would animate a crime is not more than is wanted to inspire a resolved submission, when the noble habit of the soul reasserts itself," the narrator comments, prefacing this resolution with a revealing analogy: Dorothea's struggle was like "that of a man who begins with a movement toward striking and ends with conquering his desire to strike" (bk. 4, Chap. 4). So while she never actually is violent, the metaphors that describe her emotions are violent ones.

The most angry of Eliot's women, Gwendolen Harleth, in the last novel, *Daniel Deronda*, is a distinct contrast to Dorothea. Gwendolen is prevented from committing murder by the highly coincidental drowning of her detested and abusive husband, Grandcourt. Before the dramatic denouement, she hopes he will meet with "some possible accident" for "to dwell on the benignity of accident was a refuge from worse temptation." As time passes and his tormenting increases, her thought turns to "white-lipped, fierce-eyed temptations with murdering fingers" (chap. 54). Nevertheless, she wishes, above all, to keep from being "wicked," by which she and the reader understand "murderous."

The narrator, in commenting on Gwendolen's great hatred and her dread of the intensity of her rage, observes that the "intensest form of hatred is that rooted in fear, which . . . drives vehemence into a constructive vindictiveness, an imaginary annihilation of the detested object, something like the hidden rites of vengeance with which the persecuted have made a dark vent for their rage, and soothed their suffering into dumbness" (chap. 54). But Gwendolen is not soothed by her hatred; she is inflamed. After Grandcourt is dead, she cries out: "I wanted to kill him—it was as strong as a thirst" (chap. 56).

Gwendolen is more intelligent than Caterina, more worldly, more resolute than Janet in responding to abuse. Grandcourt is also a more formidable foe, and the couple is locked in a battle of wills from their first encounter. He intends to dominate absolutely and has the advantage of understanding her "better than she understands herself, or him, or the pressures to which she is subject."[15] And there is a third party, Daniel Deronda, of whom Grandcourt is jealous and Gwendolen admiring. Thus the complexity of motive and action is increased, and Eliot, who is so tolerant of Caterina and so sympathetic to Janet, here takes an ambivalent position, as she did toward Hetty. The effect, however, is to make Gwendolen's urge to murder that much more real.[16]

Gwendolen, like Caterina, is able to confess her feelings of hatred and guilt after her husband's death. But Deronda, unlike Gilfil, is neither completely convinced of Gwendolen's innocence nor willing to comfort and support her. Gwendolen insists that a critical element of her insidious hatred was her sense of isolation. In that way she resembles Hetty and most fictional women criminals; they are cut off from anyone in whom they can confide. She (and they) believe that their feelings, particularly their hatreds, are abnormal and go beyond what anyone else could understand. Eliot had made this point before, stressing repeatedly the tragic consequences of society's denial that hatred is normal, particularly in oppressed women. It is equally potent here.

Gwendolen's frustration over past isolation and dread of future loneliness are legitimate. Deronda is not capable of understand-

W.L. Taylor's aristocratic and detached image of Gwendolen Harleth contradicts the guilty complicity she feels in the text of *Daniel Deronda;* she has willed Grandcourt's death, not watched it passively. Like other illustrators, Taylor ignored women's violent potential.

ing, or is too afraid of the implications, as she explains Grand-court's death during a sailing trip he had forced upon her: "I knew no way of killing him there, but *I did, I did kill him in my thoughts.* . . . The evil longings, the evil prayers came again and blotted everything else dim, till, in the midst of them—I don't know how it was—he was turning the sail—there was a gust—he was struck—I know nothing—*I only know that I saw my wish outside me*" (chap. 56, my italics). Gwendolen goes on: "My heart said, 'Die!'—and he sank." The moment she realized he was dead, she lost her own resolve. Too late, she shrank from her "crime." But he had already drowned. She does not know how to differentiate her desire to kill from actual murder.

Neither does Deronda. He tries to persuade her that "imagi-nation" and "thought" are not criminal if the temptation is resisted. Legally he is right. But he is not particularly persua-sive, either to Gwendolen or to himself. His assertion that she is guilty only in conscience, in assuming that her desire had the nature of action, is undercut by his own subconscious dread of her power.

Gwendolen's respected social position, and the fact that she was found floating in the water after the accident, combine to protect her from suspicion and from the need to explain the circumstances of her husband's death to the police. But she is transformed by her sense of guilt at her own capacity for violence, by what the narrator explicitly calls her "criminal desire." Her grief is intensified because she is forced to acknowl-edge that Deronda is lost to her as well, that she has killed whatever dim chance there was of an enduring relationship between them. When she collapses on the hotel-room floor after his departure, the narrator's ironic comment—"Such grief seemed natural in a poor lady whose husband had been drowned in her presence"—makes the underlying sexual tension explicit.

Undeniably, Gwendolen's desire to kill Grandcourt is inex-tricably bound up with his death, and Eliot leaves the moment of dying so deliberately ambiguous that the relative roles of pure accident and willed death are blurred. But she has made Gwendolen's fascination with violence obvious from early in the novel. One example is her "infelonious murder," strangling her sister's pet bird because its singing annoys her. Eliot also ties Gwendolen's assertive, even aggressive, behavior to the mythic image of the virgin huntress. Her skill at archery, love of riding, excitement at the hunt, and the purifying "bath" she takes by jumping into the sea after Grandcourt's death exemplify Sir Hugo Mallinger's description of her as a "perfect Diana." Her wish to dominate is expressed most cogently in a clear allusion not to Artemis (the Greek Diana), but to Artemis's twin brother, the god Apollo: Gwendolen "wished to mount the Chariot and drive the plunging horses herself, with a spouse . . . who would fold his arms and give her his countenance without looking ridiculous" (chap. 13). It was hardly the conventional Victorian view of ideal womanhood.

Gwendolen, though sometimes baffled by her own feelings, explains her passion for archery by saying that there is nothing she loves more than "taking aim—and hitting." After her marriage, she abandons the symbolic bow and arrow for a stolen dagger kept locked in her jewelry case from the first days of her honeymoon. She keeps it because she burns to kill Grandcourt, yet she locks it up and throws away the key because she fears that she will use it.

Gwendolen's destructive nature is also suggested in Eliot's serpentine imagery; her demonic potential is associated with her appearance, for her beauty is that of a sylph, a Lamia, a mermaid—beautiful and dangerous. In the novel's opening scene, she is described as "the Nereid in sea-green robes and silver ornaments, with a pale sea-green feather . . . falling over her light brown hair," an "ensemble du serpent" (chap. 1). Each time her clothing is described, the sea-green motif is continued; "pale green velvet and poisoned diamonds" clothe her public image. Her hair, beautifully dressed, is wound into heavy, ultimately threatening, coils in an extension of the subtle but frightening power of the serpent and mermaid imagery discussed in great depth by Nina Auerbach and Elisabeth Gitter.[17]

This combination of seductive beauty and aggression is most potent when Gwendolen sees Grandcourt to his watery death. He knew, as she did, that she might have tried to rescue him and did not. Her power and determination, aided by accidental advantage, are ultimately greater than his. Because he so clearly deserves an even worse fate, not only for his abuse of Gwendolen but for his arrogant and inhumane treatment of Lydia Glasher and their children, Eliot comes very close to advocating murder. Indeed, because Gwendolen lives to become a better—if chastened—person, Grandcourt's death has positive consequences.

There is more to Grandcourt's death, however. The sexual tension implicit in Gwendolen's hatred of her husband also explains her desire to have him die. Repulsed before her marriage by expressions of passion and revolted by physical contact with men, she had convinced herself that one reason to accept Grandcourt (in addition to his money) was that he did not touch her before the wedding. Her panicky hysterics the first night of their honeymoon, triggered by a threat from Grandcourt's mistress, are clearly the result of appalling sexual ignorance.[18] Coupled with that ignorance is her recognition that sex is another weapon—like money and physical strength—in the arsenal men use against women.

Though she learned to "overcome her repugnance to certain facts" (chap. 54), her hatred for Grandcourt grows during their intolerable marriage. Her sense of being used sexually as well as abused psychologically is an added impetus to kill. Nowhere is that feeling clearer than when she sees Grandcourt ride past Lydia Glasher and his son in the park, pretending that he does not see them, for she feels a sense of community with the abandoned mistress.[19] Undeniably, too, the attraction she feels for Deronda buttresses her urgent desire to have Grandcourt dead.

But that does not mean, as Victorian convention and Victorian criminology would have it, that she killed her husband because of sexual aberration. While Eliot connects this woman's violence to sexual conflict more explicitly than she does elsewhere, sexual emotions are only part of Gwendolen's motives, and they are closely linked to her loss of independence and realization of powerlessness. Those feelings, Eliot makes clear, are completely rational and sympathetic. In that way sexuality is made normal, or natural, for women just as rage and violence (and crime) are.

Despite Gwendolen's potential for violence and her motive for murder, Eliot does limit her literal guilt. Carol Christ argues that this diminishes the novel's realism and the heroine's tragic potential because Eliot is unwilling to confront the consequences of actual physical aggression.[20] But Gwendolen's culpability is perfectly clear and her ability to survive, to grow as the result of her suffering, is a radical rejection of the inevitable death or madness with which Eliot's contemporary novelists punished their guilty women. If it was not right to kill an abusive man, it was at least overwhelmingly sympathetic.

FIVE

Mary Elizabeth Braddon: The Most Despicable of Her Sex

The women who shoot, poison, stab, steal, and blackmail their way through the sensation novels of the 1800s changed the nature of crime and criminals in Victorian fiction. These women are more ambitiously independent and less sexually repressed than traditional heroines, and their criminality is pervasive, violent, and even bizarre. Like comparable characters in other Victorian literature, they reaffirm the nineteenth-century precept that female sexuality and criminality are inextricably intertwined. But they also introduce the revolutionary idea that women are capable of committing almost any crime to achieve their personal goals. Ironically, those goals are almost always highly conventional: romantic happiness and financial security through marriage.

While the criminal women in sensation fiction are assertive and aggressive, they are rarely monstrous, although Margaret Oliphant and her contemporary literary critics persistently labeled them as bestial and inhuman.[1] They do not kill (or try to kill) children or old ladies; instead they kill able-bodied men and women who threaten their plans or their well-being. Nor despite their overtly aggressive behavior, are many women in sensation fiction "masculine" in the pejorative sense that the term is applied to unconventional women. Rather, they are charming and beautiful—and sometimes quite sexy. This combination of apparent loveliness and masked threat was the most radical feature of the genre not only because it confronted the fantasy of the "angel in the house" directly but because it confirmed the worst fears of a society reluctant to admit that women were not adequately protected by the legal system and equally reluctant to change the status quo.

The audience for sensation fiction was predominantly middle class or aspiring middle class and overwhelmingly female. The unparalleled success of the genre strongly suggests that these readers clearly enjoyed being shocked and appalled—within certain well-defined parameters, of course. They relished details of the exotic, the daring, the bizarre—excitement often supplied by accusations against women in widely reported criminal trials of the 1840s, 1850s and 1860s as well as in the fiction. But the readers also came to recognize, if they had not already known, that spouse abuse or the threat of public disgrace could make a woman desperate enough to consider murder.

Partly new novels of manners and partly tales of terror, the sensation novels provided a unique blend of realism and melodrama at a time when the pervasive extent of crime in Victorian society was being explicitly reported in the press.[2] Despite their conventional, if often hollow, romantic endings, most sensation novels accurately depicted the details of Victorian society, including the overwhelming extent to which women were dependent on the authority of men and the rage which women's attempts to gain legal and economic rights evoked. Yet they shifted criminal activity from the working and indigent classes where much of it occurred to the middle and upper classes. There was no particular shock, and not much interest, generated by a housemaid killing her illegitimate baby; that was commonplace and comprehensible. And it was easy for readers to maintain a self-satisfied distance from these girls whom they expelled from their employment and ignored on the streets. In contrast, the machinations of the rich and well-born added a savory touch to violence. When a lady killed her husband, a rich girl horsewhipped a stable boy, or a clergyman's adoring daughter incited her father to murder her unfaithful lover, that was simultaneously a source of titillation and admiration.

Yet even as they described crime among the affluent and the socially prominent, the novelists deftly avoided highly sensitive issues as well as the sexual candor characteristic of contemporary French fiction. I have uncovered no novels, for example, in which middle- or upper-class women murder their illegitimate children and none with explicit incest. Such shocking crimes were too direct an assault on the Victorian obsession with family for the novelists to risk. Furthermore, few unmarried women kill. Because one underlying assumption in these novels was that passion motivated violent crime, women who were presumed sexually inexperienced could not feel passion intense enough to drive them to murder. A similiar lack of candor linked married women's violent crimes to unsatiated lust or unintentional bigamy more frequently than to actual adultery or illegitimate children.

Nor were the sensation novelists any more inclined than the authors of more traditional fiction to have their guilty women end up in a courtroom. It was perfectly all right to ask readers to believe that women murdered; many were apparently happy to have their worst fears confirmed. It was quite another to flout what the fiction's audience knew, that middle- and upper-class women were rarely caught up in the criminal justice machinery, seldom convicted, and never executed. But the novelists also avoided court trials because they preferred extrajudicial resolutions where fictional women inevitably suffered stringent, sometimes self-inflicted punishment, often in marked contrast to male characters of comparable guilt.

For instance, Philip Sheldon, the grasping and murderous antagonist of Mary Elizabeth Braddon's *Birds of Prey* and *Charlotte's Inheritance*, literally gets away with murder as he grows enormously rich at others' expense. He pays no penalty for his crimes because he is never caught and has no conscience to bother him. But women characters are destroyed for a single crime: Sylvia Perriam in Braddon's *Taken at the Flood* dies a miserable, lonely death for committing her aged husband to an insane asylum and pretending he was dead so she could bigamously marry her lover, and Honora Grace in A.M. Meadows's *The Eye of Fate* is incarcerated in an insane asylum for killing the man who had rejected her. While neither woman is sympathetic, neither is more culpable than Sheldon. And although Braddon makes Sheldon's success a clear and damning miscarriage of justice, she does not permit any of her guilty women to escape punishment as she does him. This curious inversion of real life—where men were more apt to be imprisoned or executed than women—underlines the highly conventional moral tone of a genre widely condemned as disreputable and immoral.

Finally, there is a striking disparity in the motives of the privileged women who commit crimes in sensation fiction— except in response to physical abuse—and the motives of less affluent women who in real life were more apt to be violent, or at least to be arrested for violence. Repeatedly, in fiction, the urgency to maintain her reputation and the security that reputation provides drive an otherwise conventional woman to crime more often than need or greed. Nowhere is that better illustrated than in *Lady Audley's Secret*, the archetypal sensation novel, where maintaining the secrets of the past are Lucy Audley's motive for murder: The men she attacks know or suspect the truth about her and threaten to expose her. The same motive holds true in novels and stories where women are set up as suspects in murder cases and ultimately cleared—like Aurora Floyd in Braddon's eponymous novel, or Kate Gaunt in Charles Reade's *Griffith Gaunt*, or Grace Dunbar in Conan Doyle's "The Adventure of Thor Bridge." The presumptive motive is fear that their extramarital liaisons will be exposed.

In some sensation novels, a woman's ambition for money, power, or a particular man makes her turn to the efficiency of murder rather than relying on the more insidious, but more ladylike, psychological emasculation characteristic of more conventionally destructive women. In A.M. Meadows's *Ticket of Leave Girl*, Wilkie Collins's *The Legacy of Cain*, and several of Braddon's later novels, women commit murder without the slightest qualm and acknowledge their guilt only when confronted with incontrovertible evidence. Should someone else be punished in their place, their only response, we are led to

believe, would be a sigh of relief. Unsympathetic and ultimately
unsuccessful, these women nonetheless demonstrate one of the
cardinal principles of the sensation fiction genre: women are
capable of calculated and violent action when it serves their
purpose.

The other direct assault sensation fiction made on its chauvinistic and xenophobic readers was that the guilty women were
clearly and undeniably English. Unlike Dickens, whose killers
were Europeans, or Conan Doyle, who was partial to Americans,
Australians, Russians, or almost anyone "foreign," Braddon,
Reade, Collins, and their colleagues had no reservations about
hiding a criminal mind behind a pretty English face. Blonde
curls and large blue eyes do not necessarily signal placidity and
compliance any more than an elevated social position guarantees
compassion and tolerance. In fact, after reading a few Braddon
novels, the reader grows very wary of beautiful rich women.

No novel about female violence made a more dramatic impact
than Braddon's first best-seller, *Lady Audley's Secret* (1862).
Lucy Audley's violations of Victorian moral and legal codes in
her quest for emotional and financial security are monumental:
when her first husband, George Talboys, disappears, leaving no
word of his plans or whereabouts, she abandons her child,
assumes a false identity, gets a job, and marries Sir Michael
Audley bigamously. When Talboys returns, she fakes an obitu-
ary, stages her own funeral, attempts murder, and commits
arson. The reader must marvel at her energy and ingenuity.

Elaine Showalter suggests that Lucy nearly gets away with
her treachery because her innocent looks place her above suspicion.[3] Yet her skills at dissembling learned as woman/wife
make her capable not only of deception but of putting her own
happiness and success above all other considerations, legal or
moral. In addition, Lucy Audley combines classically feminine
assets—a beautiful face and an outwardly gentle manner—with
a distinctly unfeminine one—her resourceful mind. To be sure
that no reader misses the point that Lucy is guilty, Braddon
uses the admittedly clichéd but extremely effective device of
describing her portrait, stressing the strange, almost demonic,
quality of her beauty while hinting at a sinister aspect of its

loveliness: "Her crimson dress, exaggerated like all the rest in this strange picture, hung about her in folds that looked like flames, her fair head peeping out of the lurid mass of color as if out of a raging furnace. Indeed the crimson dress, the sunshine on the face, the red gold gleaming in the yellow hair, the ripe scarlet of the pouting lips, the glowing colors of each accessory of the minutely painted background, all combined to render the first effect of the painting by no means an agreeable one" (chap. 8).[4]

Robert Audley, a dilettante obsessed with his uncle's wife and his friend Talboys's second disappearance, has the most visceral reaction. For him, the portrait stirs subconscious images of Lucy as a predator and helps convince him she is guilty of some horrible if undefined evil. It also strengthens his resolve to make her pay for her sins—if only he can find out what they are. He dreams of her as a mermaid, "beckoning his uncle to destruction" (chap. 27) and as a Medusa, whose golden ringlets change into snakes and crawl down her neck, threatening the dreamer himself (chap. 13). These conventional Victorian images of feminine power and masculine dread tell the reader as much about Robert Audley as they do about the woman he sees as the personification of evil. But in this context, the golden web of Lucy's hair evokes not only the insidious destructive power that her nephew fears but also the obsession with being rich that has motivated her dishonest marriage.[5]

Lucy Audley's crimes are of two kinds: the careful, crafted deceits which create her new persona and bury her past, and the spontaneous, violent actions to get rid of the two men— George Talboys and Robert Audley—who can destroy her. She pushes Talboys down an abandoned well and leaves him to die. To cover up that crime, she sets fire to the inn where Audley is staying while he investigates her past. Her motive each time is self-defense, but what she is protecting is not her life but her reputation. That reputation as an innocent, helpless, and virtuous woman is what insures her social position and her hard-won security. She threatens, she uses physical force in wanton disregard for human life, and she believes she has committed murder but feels no remorse. As a killer, however, she is a

Robert Audley attributes the sinister beauty of Lady Audley's revealing portrait to some unnamed Pre-Raphaelite. Edward Burne-Jones captures that quality in his portrait of the seductress Sidonia von Bork. Courtesy of the Tate Gallery, London, and Art Resource, New York.

failure; neither man dies. So why does Braddon punish her? Why does Lucy Audley die in an insane asylum? And why, for many readers, does she get what she deserves?

The answer lies in Lucy's refusal to accept her plight as a poor daughter, an abandoned wife, or a penniless governess, when everything she has learned teaches her that a woman's success is measured by an affluent marriage. The bigamy (with its overtones of sexual excess) which is her undoing enables her to marry well and achieve the financial security that neither her father nor Talboys provided. The luxury she craves is guaranteed by being a rich man's wife: having expensive clothes, sumptuous surroundings, a life of ease. She has no objection to marriage, no ambitions for a career, no wish to be independent. She relishes her new position and swears that her strongest desire is to be Sir Michael's faithful and devoted wife.

Robert Audley, as he tightens the web of evidence in which he plans to trap her, is frightened by her violence but absolutely repelled by her resourcefulness in deceiving all of them for so long. Putting her at the end of a long line of deceitful women, he recalls "the horrible things that have been done by women since that day upon which Eve was created" and shudders at Lucy Audley's "hellish power of dissimulation" (chap. 29). Not content with comparing Lucy's behavior to the mythic evil of Eve and the legendary crimes of Lucrezia Borgia, Catherine de Médicis, and the Marquise de Pompadour, Robert Audley also invokes the contemporary personification of feminine deceit, Maria Manning, who had been Dickens's source for the murderous lady's maid in *Bleak House.*

Audley's reaction echoes both the general Victorian dread of women's demonic powers and the inescapable seductive appeal of a woman like Lucy.[6] Young Audley's growing revulsion at and vindictiveness toward his aunt's behavior are fueled by his initial attraction to her, and the intensity of his hatred is set against the adoration he would have felt had she been as sweet and docile as she seemed. It is very much to the point that the once-assertive woman he ends up marrying meekly abandons her independence for domestic bliss, exactly as everyone thinks Lucy has done.

Lucy, after all, is correct in her assessment that a woman's security is determined by how well she marries, but ironically neither of Lucy's husbands defends or protects her when she is in need and neither assumes responsibility for the events which precipitate her self-protecting violence. Talboys abandons her and their child, penniless, without warning or explanation. He sends no word for three years. Yet it never occurs to him that he has done anything wrong or that she will not be waiting patiently when he returns. Later, Sir Michael walks away from her when her bigamy is revealed, all his "love" gone. The anguish he feels is for himself, not for her, though her plea for forgiveness makes clear that she anticipates the grim fate which awaits her.

The other men in the novel are no more protective. Lucy's father is an incompetent drunk; Robert Audley is a vindictive meddler who can never keep his motives straight; and Luke Marks is a shiftless, ruthless blackmailer who knows no murder has been committed and yet profits from Lady Audley's dread of discovery. No one forces her, of course, to use violence to cover her deceits, as no one had forced her to measure success in materialistic terms. The reason she is punished so cruelly is that she has somehow bested men—or so they believe. Braddon implies that they do not want justice as much as they want revenge.

When Robert Audley confronts Lucy with the results of his investigations, he calls her "an artful woman . . . a bold woman . . . a wicked woman." He concludes this diatribe with an accusation that would be ludicrous if he were not so serious: "If this woman of whom I speak had never been guilty of any blacker sin that the publication of that lying announcement [of her own death] in the *Times* newspaper, I should still hold her as the most detestable and despicable of her sex—the most pitiless and calculating of creatures. That cruel lie was a base and cowardly blow in the dark, it was the treacherous dagger-thrust of an infamous assassin" (chap. 29).

And he is not finished: "Do you think the gifts which you have played against fortune are to hold you exempt from retribution? No, my lady, your youth and beauty, your grace and refinement, only make the horrible secret of your life more horrible" (chap. 29). After Lucy's confession of bigamy and hereditary insanity (purportedly the real secret she is trying to hide), Audley finds a convenient Victorian way to punish her without involving the judicial system, and without exposing her—and more importantly, his family—to the scandal of a trial.[7]

The doctor he engages insists that Lucy is not mad, yet he warns that she is dangerous. Convinced that no court in the country would convict her of either George Talboys's or Luke Marks's murder on the basis of the available evidence, he nonetheless arranges for her to be confined in a madhouse for the rest of her life. His reason? He believes—because she does not take the trouble to hide her animosity toward him, as a true lady would—that she poses a threat to society at large, the *one* charge that the narrator never makes and that none of Lucy's actions support. Elaine Showalter thinks that Braddon introduces madness to prevent Lucy from being tried, convicted, and executed for murder. In that way, Braddon could "spare her women readers the guilt of identifying with a cold-blooded killer."[8] That reading ignores the fact that Lucy could not have been brought to trial without some conclusive proof of her guilt in Talboys's second disappearance. Further, Victorian judicial history suggests that even though Lucy was responsible for Luke Marks's death, she probably would not have been tried, even more probably would not have been convicted, and certainly would not have been executed for killing a man of his class and reputation. Had she been found guilty of either arson or bigamy, the court in all probability would have committed her to an insane asylum just as Audley does.

Rather, Braddon used the insanity device because it allows Lucy Audley to be locked up—not for murder or bigamy or arson but for daring to assert some control over her own life. Her punishment enabled Robert Audley to demonstrate the authority over women that he believes men should have. By labeling Lucy "insane," he can reaffirm that sane women are dependent and need his help in dealing with the problems in their lives. There is, as well, an inescapable connection between Audley's telling himself that Lucy is insane and his letting her

step-daughter believe that Lucy has been guilty of some outrageous but unspecified sexual indiscretion. Insane women and
promiscuous women fit his, and his society's, perception of
deviant female behavior. Women who throw men down wells,
set fire to hotels, and try to strangle people with their bare
hands do not fit any comfortable Victorian's idea of how a
woman would behave.

Braddon's most serious limitation in depicting Lucy Audley
as a criminal is that her perspective is not consistent. Not only
does she switch the protagonist of the novel from Lucy to Robert
Audley partway through the story, but also her narrator's
original sympathy for Lucy gives way to open antagonism. As
a result, the narrator's comments are ruthless and sometimes
incredible in their criticism; yet Braddon surely intended the
final scene between Lucy and her "judge and jailer," Robert
Audley, to rouse the reader to profound pity for the woman.
Lucy's description of George Talboys's goading and tormenting
makes her violent response to him perfectly understandable,
perhaps even forgivable. The disproportion between the harm
she has actually caused and the punishment she suffers is
enormous. The gravest injustice of all is that Robert Audley
makes no attempt to have her released from the asylum when
he discovers that George Talboys is not dead. He is instead
confident that "it may be some comfort to her to hear that her
husband did not perish in his youth by her wicked hand" (chap.
38).

Lady Audley was Braddon's first big success, but it was not
her last. Prolific and inventive, she changed her themes and her
characters to keep pace with the demands of popular fiction
while continuing to create women who were violent or incited
violent actions in others. Whether those books were formulaic
tales like *Taken at the Flood* (1874) or powerful analyses of
destructive emotions like *Joshua Haggard's Daughter* (1876),
Braddon used the serious social and moral issues implicit in
crime to produce a radical if circumspect attack on Victorian
self-esteem. In the latter novel, a clergyman, his daughter, and
his much-younger bride are caught in a web of jealousy, wife
abuse, and subliminal incest which results in the murder of the

daughter's fiancé and the consequent deaths of Haggard and his wife. Naomi Haggard, whose jealous fury provokes her father to murder, single-mindedly devotes herself to sustaining her father's saintly reputation, although she is fully aware of his guilt and her own complicity. Braddon makes clear that appearance and reality are not the same, that corruption can flourish beneath a respectable facade.

The growing frankness with which Braddon and her contemporaries describe sexual feelings (though not actions) demonstrates the liberating effect of a decade of sensation novels on English fiction. Though still far more discreet than Zola in *Thérèse Racquin* (1869) or Nikolai Leskov in "Madame Macbeth of Mzinsk" (1865) in acknowledging the power of love and hate to beget violence, Victorian novelists were increasingly candid in pointing out the consequences of frustrated emotions in otherwise quite ordinary women (and men).

Oliver Madox Brown is a case in point. In *The Black Swan*, he describes Gabriel Denver's infidelity and his wife's murderous rage as the direct consequences of sexual and emotional frustration.[9] Early in the novel Brown uses conventional imagery to describe the outraged and threatening Dorothy Denver: her teeth glisten in a dark-complected face, her deep-set eyes, "glittering with the revengeful reckless light of madness," make her look diabolical, and the overall impression is that of "an enraged venomous snake" (chap. 1). As the novel unfolds, though, Dorothy becomes less a symbol of evil and more an obsessed woman determined to punish the lovers for her private agony and public embarrassment.

Denver himself recognizes the legitimacy of Dorothy's rage, not only in feeling guilty about the passion he cannot control but also about the hollow emptiness in the life they had shared as man and wife. He freely admits that he married Dorothy for her money and held her at arm's length until she abandoned any attempts to please him or to break through his reserve. "What psychologist," Denver muses, "can fathom . . . the soul of a neglected woman, hardened into strange formations of dull, callous feeling?" (chap. 4). As a result, the more Denver's active hatred for his wife becomes apparent, the more ambivalent the

reader becomes about his motives for loving Laura and about
Dorothy's justification for wanting to punish them. It is enough,
in James Ashcroft Noble's words "to leave a sense of jarring
discord between our judgment and our emotions."[10]

An abandoned woman, far from home, without the comfort
of children, family, or friends might, in a more conventional
novel, have taken to her bed with an attack of brain fever. But
not Dorothy Denver. Before she finally sets fire to the ship on
which they are traveling and precipitates all their deaths, she
threatens to murder both her husband and his beloved Laura.
"I could have struck a knife into your hearts!" she shouts at
him. "I'll strangle you in your sleep!" (chap. 1).

Dorothy's rage does not make her a heroine, even in an
unconventional sense. Physically and morally unattractive, she
is a cold-blooded killer, outraged that she does not live long
enough to see her enemy die. Indeed she becomes nearly
hysterical as the weakened and dehydrated Laura goes on
breathing: "Not dead yet? is she always to live on and make my
eyesight a curse to me? What have I done to kill and destroy
her, that she still lingers there like a starved snake? Oh God! if
it's useless after all, and I've given my soul to hell and my body
to death only to be cheated! I'll strangle her sooner myself"
(chap. 8). This otherwise ordinary Englishwoman commits a
crime of such magnitude, of such reckless disregard for the lives
of innocent sailors, of such total destruction, that the reader is
jolted by the import of her dying words: "I told you you should
learn what a woman's love turned to hatred could do" (chap. 8).

Brown is morally conventional in having the guilty Dorothy
die a miserable death: the "burning" triggered by the madness
of drinking sea water is a none too subtle reflection of her burning
hate and the burning ship. It suited Victorian sensibility that
she destroys herself by the violence she uses against others.
But the novel's jarring power comes from the explosion of
emotions which escape from her tightly reined control, a control
which Dickens feared because it was so vulnerable to stress,
and Eliot advocated because women without it were destructive.
Brown's novel is not a plea for more liberal divorce laws nor a
moral judgment on loveless marriages and infidelity, but an

examination of the internal and external forces which can unite to drive usually conventional, even ordinary, women to gruesome crimes.

Helen Mathers, another popular late-Victorian novelist who regularly cast women criminals as major characters, is the author of a particularly sympathetic and sensitive examination of intertwined passion and guilt: *Murder or Manslaughter* (1885). The novel, which foreshadows the tragedy of Thomas Hardy's *Tess of the D'Urbervilles*, tells the story of the hapless Beryl Booth. Charged with murdering her husband because of the rumor that she was having an illicit love affair at the time of his death, Beryl initially confesses. Lacking the will to defend herself in court because she believes herself responsible for his death, she only reluctantly agrees to allow Hugo Holt, the man she loves, to mount a daring refutation of the charges. Then, when he seems to have convinced the court that the death was a suicide, she cries out that the defense is a lie, that she did meet her lover in the garden, that she meant "to take a human life," and that she deserves to die. The jury, taking her at her word, convicts her and she is sentenced to hang.

She holds herself at fault on two counts: before her husband's death she had confessed to him her passionate attraction to the brilliant attorney, and she had bought the poison her husband drank, intending to take it herself because she could think of no other escape. In her own mind she is as guilty as if she had stabbed him through the heart, although she knows perfectly well that Holt's suicide defense is sound. The underlying issue, as it so often is in novels with women killers, is the guilt attached to extramarital love, even when that love is unconsummated. On that subject Mathers is brilliant, both in evoking the lovers' awakening mutual passion and in dissecting Beryl's obsessive self-denial, initially resisting the truth about her feelings and then rejecting the physical and emotional fulfillment of a love affair because she has internalized the moral values of her time and place.

Like the most perceptive novelists of the period, Mathers is candid about women's craving for satisfying emotional (and romantic) relationships, men's profound chauvinism, and the trap a hollow marriage becomes for women who crave more than financial security and social position. What is more unusual is that moral rectitude is not the only reason Beryl Booth resists adultery; if it were, the modern reader would be less touched by her struggle. Rather, as a woman who has established her own persona through popular success as a painter, she refuses to become any man's mistress. She knows all too well that Holt has no intention of creating a scandal or risking his own reputation by leaving his wife to live openly with her. In fact he says as much. Yet he begs her to do what he will not, to move into the demimonde. And she resents it.

Other evidence of the novelist's serious purpose is found in Mathers's creative use of standard sensation novel devices. For instance, the painting in *Lady Audley's Secret* which suggested some sinister force behind a benign facade is hard to take seriously as character development. But when Beryl Booth, desperately unhappy, paints a domestic scene labeled "Deserted," with her husband hovering between sleep and death while she herself watches impassively from the doorway, there is little doubt that the work echoes the turmoil in her own mind. And when the painting is used during her trial as evidence that the murder was premeditated, the reader can quarrel only with the interpretation. That it reveals something about the psychological state of its creator is never in doubt.

Similarly, the recurrent references to physical abuse are not used for shock effect; in fact, violence never actually occurs. Instead the threats of violence comment on the dynamic of a romantic relationship in which a man (in this case Hugo Holt) expects to have his own way and is denied. On two different occasions he threatens to beat Beryl for resisting his advances. The suggestion, of course, is that he could force her to bend to his will. And though he never strikes her, there is an element of real menace in his words, a threat that grows out of his frustration, that seems to him within the limits of tolerance, and is kept in check only by his own force of will.

Finally, the opposition between a virtuous woman and a shameless adventuress, which is so often the centerpiece of nineteenth-century fiction, is given an ironic twist in *Murder or*

Manslaughter. The "guilty" woman is not temptress but tempted. Her husband is so obsessed with his scientific investigations that he has little time for her, though she is eager to be a good wife. Her lover importunes her to no avail. She believes her friends when they insist that men have all the pleasures in love and women all the penalties. And Holt's wife is dull and shallow by comparison with the object of his desire: "Serenely unconscious of rivalry, but fully aware of her advantages, which included her house, her diamonds, her gaieties, her children, and, last of all, her husband, Mrs. Holt looked exactly like what she was—a handsome, well-meaning, good sort of second rate woman" (chap. 37).

But Mathers, like her heroine, was finally a woman of her time, and, in the crunch, virtue, not independence, was the theme she chose to stress. Nowhere is this clearer than after Edmund Booth's death when betrayal is no longer a bar to Beryl's liaison with Holt. Yet Beryl craves punishment, either overtly, for murder, or more ineluctably by running away after she is cleared. Who, the frustrated reader wonders, could have blamed her for staying and taking her chances at happiness with Holt? Yet for all its moralizing, the denouement is more intellectually satisfying than the resolution of Eliot's *Middlemarch*, wherein Dorothea's second marriage reduces her to conventional wifehood. Beryl Booth refuses to yield either body or soul, so although she is lonesome, she is free.

The excesses of sensation fiction had been unfairly maligned and its contributions correspondingly ignored until renewed interest in popular literature, specifically what Victorian women read and wrote, prompted reexamination of the texts.[11] It remains a valid criticism that the frequency with which women are guilty of violent crime stretches the truth, as does the emphasis on the criminality of the middle class. Yet only a hypocrite or a fool would deny that crime was omnipresent in the Victorian world or that it was often engendered by the moral and legal rigidity on which that society prided itself. In the interest of either good taste or good sales, the novelists avoided Kate Webster and her crime (chopping up her employer and cooking the pieces) and the more horrible aspects of baby-

farming and infanticide which were all too frequent in working-
class and impoverished environments and which contemporary
journalists described in gory detail. Similarly, they ignored
incest and other sexual "perversions" like homosexuality and
sadomasochism. Rather, the crimes the novels describe addressed timely issues. For instance, some of the women killers
are truly evil, and their crimes show a malevolence that goes
far beyond the bounds of rational behavior. Yet because they
maintain an aura of gentility and decorum, they are protected,
if only temporarily, from suspicion. Just as emphatically as the
novelists wanted to show women capable of anything including
murder, they wanted to expose the hypocrisy of equating con-
ventionality with moral virtue.

As a result of its candor and boldness, the sensation genre
exerted a strong influence on Victorian fiction at large, although
many contemporary novelists declared themselves appalled and
shocked by its style and subjects. George Eliot, for instance,
believed her own account of the situations which provoked women
to violence, and the cultural imperatives that kept them from
it, was more honest than what Braddon or Collins had to say.
But between Hetty Sorrel (in 1859 before the sensation era
began) and Gwendolen Harleth (after it had begun to wane in
1876) an enormous change occurred in Eliot's—and in society's—
conception of the kind of woman who could commit murder.[12]

SIX

Wilkie Collins: No Deliverance but in Death

Wilkie Collins, writing in the same decade and same genre as Braddon, was bolder in creating criminal women. Using sensational elements to startle and shock, he structured his work around people rather than events at the same time that he deliberately challenged the conventions of middle-class Victorian society. His women are more realistic and their motives more complex than those of most sensation novelists, in part because he was more adept at character development. But he was also convinced that women were not only as intelligent and determined as men, but equally convulsed by the agonies of moral choice and equally capable of asocial or amoral solutions.

Questioning the Victorian convention that self-abnegating devotion to family was a woman's finest aspiration, Collins repeatedly raised the issues of women's self-protection and self-respect. Collins's women struggle in a society in which they are unequal to men politically, socially, economically, and sometimes legally. Their recurrent, "unfeminine" boldness implies that radical action offers women an option for dealing with domestic problems that the law or social custom cannot resolve.

Prominent among his concerns was the violence which stemmed from women's vulnerability in male-dominated Victorian society. His novels make clear that women's dilemmas grow out of domestic conflicts, based in the sexual tensions between them and men. Unlike romantic fiction, where men are defenders and protectors, in his work they are frequently women's adversaries. Wife abuse, for instance, which Collins uses as background material in *The Woman in White* (1860-61) and *Armadale* (1866) becomes a central theme in *Man and Wife* (1870).

Domestic violence figured prominently in the works of other Victorian novelists—not only those of Dickens and Eliot, but also Emily Brontë's *Wuthering Heights* (1847), Anne Brontë's *The Tenant of Wildfell Hall* (1848), William Makepeace Thackeray's *The Newcomes* (1854-55), and Dinah Mulloch Craik's *A Life for a Life* (1859). Sensation novels, like G.A. Lawrence's *Barren Honour* (1868), included abusive, and often drunken, husbands. But before Collins, the realistic and frightening underside of unhappy marriages was a minor theme, frequently obscured by a conventionally happy ending. Unlike his contemporaries, Collins made his women strike back. Before *Armadale*, physically abused wives died or ran away; they did not kill. Women characters who murdered men did so for other reasons, like revenge or ambition. Afterward, the moral quandaries posed by victim-precipitated violence became an increasingly common theme in fiction—in Eliot's *Daniel Deronda*, for instance, or Hardy's *Tess of the d'Urbervilles*. In one real-life adaptation of this explanation for domestic violence, Adelaide Bartlett's defense attorney combined the argument that her husband had been too sexually aggressive with the claim that she was nevertheless innocent of his death. To the court's astonishment the jury found her innocent.[1]

While he does not condone murder, literally or metaphorically, Collins repeatedly stresses the social causes of criminality—alienation, abuse, economic deprivation—and shows profound sympathy for women faced with the unpalatable choice between suffering and violence. Using crime as a metaphor for rebellion against the status quo, Collins frequently makes his women who do kill strong and resourceful. His innovation is important; with the exception of Thackeray's Becky Sharp, no woman criminal in earlier English fiction was either particularly intelligent or particularly rebellious. After Collins, they frequently were.

Winifred Hughes points out, however, that "equivocal heroines" like Collins's were denounced by Victorian literary critics as morally repulsive and held up as examples of the chief threat to the "social and moral fabric of Victorian England."[2] Because womanly demureness and dependence were seen as the cornerstones of society, and women were revered for being different from—and better than—men, the aggressive boldness of Collins's women was intolerable to many.[3] Collins also infuriated the critics by assailing the Victorian assumption that depravity was a primary cause of women's criminality. His women are undeniably sexual creatures, conscious of their own physical and emotional desires and willing to play on men's infatuation to fulfill their ambitions. But Collins is very careful to establish that neither sexual immorality nor uncontrolled sexual desire is the primary factor in any character's decision to murder.

Collins's purpose is neither to idealize women nor to denigrate them, but to stress their normalcy, even when they are criminals. While his narrators are sometimes critical of women who commit acts of violence, the motives for those crimes are always carefully defined. I have already pointed out that Collins described recurrent physical abuse as a cause for violence; the related issue of financial dependence, which resulted from the profound difficulty women experienced finding legitimate, profitable employment, also figures repeatedly in Collins's assessment of women's motives for crime.

To emphasize the seriousness of the underlying social issues implicit in women's deviance, he strove for verisimilitude in their behavior even in his most sensational novels. His women killers most often use poison rather than knives or guns, just as women did in real life. Collins also emphasizes premeditation—a necessary component of a poisoning murder but a relatively unusual theme in Victorian fiction. One reason others avoided it may have been that describing someone plotting a murder could undermine any sympathy a reader might feel for her. There may, in fact, be circumstances when stabbing a man through the heart is a more palatable murder than lacing his soup with arsenic. But Collins took the risk.

Realistic murder weapons are only one way Collins drew on real criminal cases as sources for his fiction. As many critics point out, he often adopted specific details, putting the incrimi-

nating nightgown of the Constance Kent case (which was finally
resolved in 1864) into *The Moonstone* (1868). Sometimes actual
cases which highlighted social problems or miscarriages of justice
suggested the theme of a novel, as the Susannah Palmer wife-
abuse case (1869) did for *Man and Wife* (1870). In other novels,
tidbits from spectacular cases, including the poisoning charges
against Madeline Smith and the execution of Maria Manning,
crop up randomly, along with allusions to their press coverage
and their seemingly endless fascination for the public.[4] That is,
Collins deliberately associated his criminals with notorious
women overtly at odds with Victorian mores.

Another way Collins worked for verisimilitude was to use
letters and diaries as a technique for character development. In
part a reversion to the first-person tradition of the eighteenth-
century epistolary novel, the technique was even more directly
related to the Victorian habit of voluminous correspondence and
extensive journal-keeping. In Madeleine Smith's spectacular
murder trial (1857), the most damaging evidence of her potential
(but not proven) criminality was the explicit language of her
love letters; unguarded letters also helped to convict Christiana
Edwards, Florence Maybrick, and Edith Carew of murder before
century's end. The similarly revelatory and incriminating power
of a diary had been demonstrated, as well, by the Robinson
case in 1858, when Mrs. Robinson's effusive but probably self-
deluding descriptions of her sexual liaison were the grounds for
her husband's unsuccessful divorce suit.[5]

When Collins's women speak for themselves, either in letters
or diaries, they are more assertive and direct than they are in
conversation or when their words and deeds are filtered through
the perceptions of a masculine narrator. In *Armadale* and *Man
and Wife*, for instance, women's diaries play out the conflicting
emotions and torturous decisions crucial to the planned murders,
so Lydia Gwilt and Hester Dethridge are developed more sym-
pathetically than they could otherwise be. Self-explanation,
which admittedly is sometimes strictly self-justification, here
serves the more valuable task of describing provocation and
motive from a woman's perspective. Collins ultimately over-

worked the device. In his later novels, diaries provide the only evidence of guilt, and they are often conveniently "discovered" to prove a case against a killer when the plot provides no other evidence. More disturbing, he came to accept the cliché asserting women's particular compulsion to confess. But in the earlier work internal debates between good and evil, like Lydia Gwilt's in *Armadale*, resemble the agonizing, often subconscious, torture Dostoyevsky portrays in his criminals.

As Collins became increasingly committed to using fiction as a vehicle for social criticism, he turned for source material to the debates raging in the medical and scientific communities about the causes of crime. Curiously, despite his iconoclastic treatment of heredity versus environment (in *The Legacy of Cain*) or the relationship of insanity to criminality (in *Jezebel's Daughter*), he ignored the contemporary crime theories most directly related to women—the ones that proposed biological explanations for women's violent behavior. He never suggests, as his medical contemporaries would have done, that the hallucinations that tempt Hester Dethridge to murder may be related to menopause or that Lydia Gwilt's periodic depression may be hormonally based. If it was delicacy that kept Collins from describing women's bodily functions, it is an ironic contrast to his forthright treatment of other taboo subjects, such as prostitution, which he insists was fostered by economic factors, not sexual depravity. It is more tempting to think that he rejected biomedical explanations for the same reasons they are so unpalatable today: that they are so often employed, wittingly or not, to denigrate women.

The Woman in White was Collins's first attempt to create women criminals. The protagonist is fractured into three characters: one strong and two weak. Marian Halcombe is a capable and potentially rebellious woman; her half-sister, Laura Fairlie Glyde, is an abused wife; and Laura's illegitimate half-sister, Anne Catherick, is a misused daughter. Paralleling the protagonists is a triad of female antagonists: Mrs. Rubelle and the Countess Fosco, the agents of the novel's charming villain, and Mrs. Catherick, Anne's mother, a cold and calculating woman who married one man she despised to cover up her sexual indiscretion and then blackmailed another into supporting her for life.

One important question the novel raises is who fights women's battles. And the answer—except in Mrs. Catherick's case—is that men do. Initially Marian thinks herself capable of protecting her sister from Percival Glyde; when she sees the bruise he has left on Laura's arm, she realizes she would have killed him had she been his wife: "She showed me the marks. I was past grieving over them, past crying over them, past shuddering over them. They say we are either better than men, or worse. If the temptation that has fallen in some women's way, and made them worse, had fallen in mine at that moment—Thank God! my face betrayed nothing that his wife could read. The gentle, innocent, affectionate creature thought I was frightened for her and sorry for her—and thought no more" (book. 2, chap. 7). But Marian does not kill Glyde, or Count Fosco either. She can anticipate their moves and repel their advances, but she is incapable of making them stop or forcing them to admit their guilt. Despite that frustration, she is adamant that they pay for Laura's abuse and pushes Walter Hartright toward revenge.

In the novels that followed, women take their own revenge against the abuses they suffer. They are victims of abuse like Laura and Anne, but share Marian's intelligence and Mrs. Catherick's amoral self-interest. The combination makes them formidable and almost always potentially sympathetic. None of them is more carefully developed than the spectacular Lydia Gwilt, the red-haired villainess of *Armadale*. Gwilt is an unusual protagonist for a Victorian novel, and Collins is ambivalent about her and the implications of her behavior.

Collins makes Gwilt reprehensible, as any character who plans a cold-blooded murder must be, and at the same time the most vibrant, natural, and candid character in the novel. She treats murder as an acceptable method of achieving revenge and employs her practiced sensuality to enthrall the men whose cooperation she needs for her various schemes. She sets ethical considerations aside at crucial moments and represses her guilty conscience when it inconveniently interferes with her plans. While she is resolutely amoral, Gwilt's driving motivation is identical with that of conventional Victorian heroines: the emotional and financial security provided through marriage. This passionate struggle between her willingness to kill and her craving for love is the substance of her character.

Gwilt's physical appearance reflects this duality. Her beautiful face, capped by luxuriant red hair, is the clearest evidence of her womanliness; at the same time it embodies her potential for evil. Described as "the one unpardonably remarkable shade of colour which the prejudice of the Northern nations never entirely forgives" (bk. 3, chap. 10), her hair, like her character, is "hideous" (3, 10) and "magnificent" (4,7).

Gwilt consciously, deliberately, uses her beauty to advance her schemes of revenge, fraud, and murder, likening herself to Eve in undermining men's power. She is not only more beautiful and more intelligent than the conventional fictional heroine, but she is also older and more sexually experienced. She uses the skills she has gained with great deliberation and considerable theatricality. Flattered by her smiles and her artfully discreet caresses, men acquiesce to her requests because they hope that she will repay their devotion; this adds a specifically sexual element to Gwilt's appeal which Collins makes no attempt to disguise. Her "sexy" approach is not infallible; some men are immune and others discover some sinister quality in Gwilt's behavior which turns them away from her. But when her sex appeal works, it is a powerful weapon.

In the crucial scene which begins her seduction of Ozias Midwinter, the narrator is outspokenly explicit: "Perfectly modest in her manner, possessed to perfection of the graceful restraints and refinements of a lady, she had all the allurements that feast the eye, all the Siren-invitations that seduce the sense—a subtle suggestiveness in her silence, and a sexual sorcery in her smile" (bk. 4, chap. 7).

Having worked her magic, she carefully engineers Midwinter's departure to inflame his passion and make him more vulnerable at their next encounter. Though briefly appalled by her own hypocrisy, she acknowledges the physical as well as emotional pleasure of her conquest and is candidly unembarrassed by her sexual power. Indeed, as she undresses before the mirror and swirls her hair around her naked shoulders she relishes the thought of Midwinter's being there to admire her. Though hardly bold by twentieth-century standards, Gwilt's method for learning Midwinter's secret identity—by kissing him passionately on the mouth to end his resistance—emphasizes her practiced awareness of male vulnerability.

But Gwilt deceives herself, for she is as driven by passion as the man she wants to manipulate and she wants passion to be the expression of love and devotion rather than simply a physical act. When Midwinter's lust for her is satiated and his emotional attachment to Armadale surpasses his feelings for her, Gwilt is thrown into despair.

Collins's contemporary, Mary Elizabeth Braddon, as we have seen, hid Lady Audley's true character behind a mask of delicate beauty (*Lady Audley's Secret*, 1862), and his colleague, Charles Dickens, gave the heartless Estella strikingly good looks (*Great Expectations*, 1860-61). But while the sinister aspect of Gwilt's exceptional beauty follows convention, coupling her beauty with an unusually astute and analytical mind and a highly developed cynicism is unprecedented. Unlike Lady Audley, or George Eliot's Hetty Sorrel, who delight in their prettiness for its own sake and only secondarily for the attention it brings, Gwilt considers her face and figure a marketable asset. When she invests unsuccessfully, she pragmatically cuts her losses and tries another approach—with another man.

Gwilt plans her boldest crime for financial gain. It involves not only fraud but the unprovoked murder of an essentially harmless, if rather annoying, young man. Her scheme forces the reader to think of her not as a victim striking back but as a desperate woman grasping for security. On the other hand, she makes the choices she does partially because of the failure her life has been. The question Collins raises in the book's introduction persists: is Lydia Gwilt reprehensible or is she a woman whose admittedly criminal behavior is the direct consequence of women's social and political inequality?

Collins maintains that Gwilt's complex and contradictory

character was developed by an equally complex and contradictory environment, a society which offered women too few opportunities and held them to too many constraints. That criminals like Lydia Gwilt are made, not born, is one of the novel's central themes. She was drawn into crime initially as a vulnerable young woman alone in the world, preyed upon by a series of unscrupulous characters eager to turn either her beauty or her brains to their own advantage. No challenging legitimate occupation offered a workable alternative. The lawyer Pedgift grudgingly acknowledges that she would have been a formidable attorney if the Bar were open to women, but it was not. And though suited by her education to be a governess, her one attempt was a resounding disaster.

Lydia did no better at marriage. She was convicted of poisoning her abusive first husband, though she was saved from execution by the power of indignant public opinion: "The verdict of the Law was reversed by general acclamation; and the verdict of the newspapers carried the day" (bk. 4, chap. 15). While Pedgift deplores this ironic, chivalric wrinkle in the Victorian reaction to women killers, contemporary readers knew perfectly well that it was predictable: no middle-class woman was likely to be executed for such a crime.

To some extent Gwilt is a liberated woman, who would be shocking even if murder were not part of her plan. What she really wants is the power to make her own decisions, find her own financial security, direct her own destiny. Yet as intensely as she wants independence, she repeatedly surrenders it because she can imagine no way to survive on her own. Though she rebels against the constraints which make women subservient, she repeatedly chooses marriage as a means to fulfillment. There is a powerful irony in Gwilt's intention of becoming Allan Armadale's widow without ever having been his wife. Widowhood, in this case, means financial security, the surest means to independence.

Despite her elaborate plans, Gwilt is a strikingly unsuccessful criminal. None of her schemes turns out as she intends: she tries to murder Armadale by masking the taste of poison with brandy; his allergy to the alcohol makes him drop the glass. She

Lydia Gwilt's actual crimes and her seductive beauty are deliberately deemphasized in Thomas's illustrations. It is impossible to tell that she is ordering Allan Armadale's murder. *Cornhill Magazine*, 1866.

arranges for him to be murdered as sea, yet he escapes; she tries again to poison him but he changes bedrooms. In addition to being incredibly unlucky, she is plagued by an overwhelming sense of shame and guilt that disrupts her concentration at critical moments and drives her to laudanum for temporary peace. And most debilitating of all is her emotional dependence on the self-righteously moral Midwinter, who is incapable of loving her as she craves to be loved.

Collins's resolution to the complex conflict between Lydia Gwilt and her society is to have her commit suicide. But does she kill herself because she is shamed by Midwinter's goodness and wants to spare him the agony of a guilty wife, as she maintains? Has she been worn down by the emotional trauma of planning a murder that has been foiled by coincidence at every turn? Does she suspect that this time her luck has run out and she will be denounced and arrested? The answer is that Collins accepted the convention that demanded that criminal women whom society cannot punish must destroy themselves.

Barbara Gates concludes that Gwilt's suicide is the most shocking assault on Victorian sensibilities that Collins could conceive; she argues that the reading public feared suicide because it was "subversive," signalling as no other action could a total rejection of the status quo. And while she concentrates on suicide as the novelist's decision instead of as the inevitable consequence of Gwilt's character, she does comment: "Collins's novels involving suicides are not formulaic. No suicide . . . is unmotivated, nor is self-destruction divorced from the painful social conflicts that beset character."[6] Gates also stresses the ambivalent emotions that Gwilt provokes in readers, seeming both beyond redemption and at the same time redeemed by her guilty conscience and her emotional desperation.

Had Collins allowed Gwilt to survive, even though her plan to kill Armadale failed, he would have been bolder yet. Had she remained unscathed like her respectable yet totally corrupt associates, the abortionist Dr. Downward and the con artist Mrs. Oldershaw, Gwilt would have posed a more serious threat to the social order. But Collins was not ready—yet—to write a novel where a beautiful woman could make crime pay.

In *The Moonstone*, Wilkie Collins retreated from the outrage evoked by Lydia Gwilt and provided a mid-Victorian look at two women suspected of theft, not guilty of murder. However, the assumptions his investigator, Sergeant Cuff, makes about women's motives and proclivities for crime demonstrate that Collins's interest in deviant women was expanding to include the explicit impact of social class on the motives and consequences of crime.

Rosanna Spearman and Rachel Verinder are as different as two women can be. Rosanna, an unattractive, belligerent woman with a deformed body and a limited education, is a former convict who has been rehabilitated as a housemaid. She is nostalgic for her old, criminal life and insists that she never felt shame and unworthiness while she was a thief. "It was only when they taught me at the Reformatory to feel my own degradation, and to try for better things, that the days grew long and weary," she explains morosely (pt. 2, chap. 4). Rachel, in contrast, is beautiful, rich, and full of enthusiasm for life. Theft and murder are totally alien to her experience, but in an ironic sense her encounter with them transforms her from a child to a resolute woman.

To Sergeant Cuff, the London detective hired to solve the mystery of Rachel's missing diamond, the heiress is as guilty as the felon-turned-housemaid. The motive is as clear to him as the culprits are. He believes Rachel got rid of the diamond because she needed ready cash to pay off debts she wanted to keep secret from her mother. She has run up gambling debts, he suggests, or must pay for some "needed service" on which he does not elaborate but which seems a clear allusion to an illicit abortion. Furthermore, he clearly implies that her crime is not at all unusual. Cuff's view is that women—including upper-class women—customarily steal if they need money, regardless of their social standing and position. In fact, he seems to blame Rosanna's backsliding into crime on Rachel too. The maid's skills as a fence, he asserts, would be useful in getting rid of the diamond once it had disappeared. Cuff insists that most convicted working-class women "go straight" if they receive kind treatment in domestic service as Rosanna has; thus, in his mind, Rachel is guilty not only of stealing her own gem to pay for her sins, but also of selfishly leading Rosanna back into a life of crime by using her contacts with the underworld.[7]

Cuff is antagonistic to Rachel not only because of her deliberately suspicious and provocative behavior, but because she does not behave as he believes a lady ought to. He resents her arrogance and despises her power to frustrate his investigations. While he is blunt—even insulting—with Rosanna, his ego is not bruised when he talks to her; thus, he is more flexible in his judgments. The class distinctions between the two women work the opposite way for the Verinder employees; unlike Cuff, they are willing to condemn the working girl rather than the lady. The principal narrator, the butler Bettridge, categorically refuses to believe any of Cuff's accusations of Rachel. It is inconceivable to him that she is guilty. And while he has been kind to Rosanna and gone out of his way to accommodate her strange behavior, he accepts her guilt when she emerges shaken and white from her interview with Cuff. His conclusion is also class based: he blames her crime on her inappropriate infatuation with Franklin Blake rather than on the influence of her former life. The unhappy conclusion of these suspicions, compounded by Blake's rejection, is that Rosanna drowns herself.

The doomed Rosanna is a particular criminal type, one for whom Collins felt a great deal of sympathy. As the illegitimate child of a prostitute whose "gentleman" deserted her, Rosanna is "typical" in the sense that her social and economic environment has been conducive to a life of crime. In addition, she has been robbed of love and attention, including the love of the father whom she has never met. Surely her yearning for paternal affection explains her attachment to Bettridge as a father-figure and also her passion for Franklin Blake, which is a combination of sexual passion and hero-worship. Her deprivations, in combination with her physical deformity, label her an outsider and contribute to her paranoia, her sense of alienation, and her frustrated passion. Collins never suggests that her feelings are unjustified; rather he makes them the background for her criminal career and the direct cause of her ultimate self-destruction.

Collins is playing games with the reader's moral judgment. On the one hand, Rosanna is unfairly accused of theft on the basis of her past life, ungainly body, and "strangeness." She is driven to suicide by others' suspicions and her own alienation. Yet Rosanna's willingness to cover up what she thinks is Blake's guilt by stealing the incriminating nightgown and her pride in her old career are explicit in the suicide letter she leaves for him: "In the days when I was a thief, I had run fifty times greater risks, and found my way out of difficulties to which *this* difficulty was mere child's play. I had been apprenticed, as you may say, to frauds and deceptions—some of them on such a grand scale, and managed so cleverly, that they became famous, and appeared in the newspapers. Was such a little thing as the keeping of the nightgown likely to weigh on my spirits. . . . What nonsense to ask that question!" (pt. 2, chap. 4).

Rachel is both more conventional than Rosanna and more appealing to Collins' middle-class audience. She is a classic heroine—virtuous and ultimately happily married. But she is also unusual; the lawyer Bruff—who loves her like a daughter—finds her independence perplexing. Rachel's boldness provides a stark contrast to Rosanna's despair. The advantages of wealth, beauty, and determination allow her to squelch the suspicions that hover around her. Collins's message is clear: women, if they are to survive, must save themselves. It was a theme to which he returned, with some startling innovations, in *Man and Wife*.

That novel's dramatic theme—that wife abuse cuts across class and age barriers and encompasses not only violence but also legal manipulation and social persecution—suggests that murder may be the only way for women to save themselves. To arrive at this radical conclusion, Collins describes several unhappy marriages—always stressing that women suffer more from marital discord than men do. In particular he dramatizes the dilemma which plagued abused wives: the impossibility of obtaining protection from their husbands through court-enforced legal separations, and the difficulty in supporting themselves when forced to earn their own living.

There are three unhappy wives in this novel: the heroine, Anne Silvester Delamayn, her mother, Anne Silvester, and the cook, Hester Dethridge. While both Anne and her mother show flashes of rage at their situation, neither murders. Clearly it takes a particular kind of woman to strike back, a woman like Hester Dethridge, whose torture extends over a protracted period of time and who finally refuses to tolerate any more misery. Collins is attentive here to the impact of personality and class on behavior; while working-class Hester grows more assertive as she is forced to deal with her miserable marriage, middle-class Anne becomes increasingly passive and withdrawn.

But the similarities between different social groups in terms of domestic violence are more striking here than their differences. While Collins is sensitive to the more overt suffering in the working class, where women without family or political connections have less opportunity to change their circumstances, he insists that there are victims of domestic violence throughout Victorian society.[8] The Dethridges' story, for example, epitomizes working-class abuse: physical violence, drunkenness, exploitation, and emotional torture. Yet the same elements, in an only slightly more refined way, characterize the Delamayn marriage. Like Joel Dethridge, Geoffrey Delamayn is a reprobate, the kind of man who kicks a dog because its barking annoys him. He is also profligate, arrogant, and greedy. Delamayn drinks too much and restrains Anne's freedom by holding her a virtual prisoner in their home.

But at least as vitriolic as Collins's attack on individual men is his assault on the laws of a supposedly civilized country which offer women no protection. In Victorian England, the legal remedies for unworkable marriages were divorce and death. A divorce, as Collins and his readers were well aware, was extremely difficult to obtain. The Matrimonial Causes Act of 1857 established civil authority for divorce actions, but made the conditions under which women could win a legal case much more stringent than for men. Furthermore, the cost was prohibitively high, so that the majority of the population (especially women) could not afford to bring suit. And though divorce was difficult, death was no more reliable—except in fiction, where novelists conveniently killed off unsuitable spouses.

Hester Dethridge's story, the tale of an industrious and virtuous wife abused by a lazy, drunken husband, is not only pathetic but based specifically on a contemporary case. During Christmas week of 1868, a woman named Susannah Palmer was charged by her husband with assault. He declared that she had struck him in the hand with a kitchen knife, threatening his life. She was arrested, tried, and convicted, but the court and the press (especially her most outspoken champion, the journalist and women's rights activist Frances Power Cobbe) made clear that Mrs. Palmer was the victim rather than the criminal.[9]

Testimony demonstrated that throughout her marriage, her husband had savagely beaten her, turned her out of the house at night, openly lived with a mistress, and frequently disappeared for months at a time, leaving her to support herself and her children by working as a charwoman. Periodically, however, he returned home and helped himself to her wages, sold her furniture to raise more cash, abused her physically, and disappeared again until his next visit. Under the law, he had every right to her property and she had no right to a divorce. Nor were there any legal provisions that could effectively protect her from beating. The law said he could be fined, whipped, or jailed if she complained that he abused her. But there was no way to prevent him from returning home if he chose to do so—and he chose to come often enough to avoid being charged with desertion.

In transforming Palmer's misery into fiction, Collins elaborates in great detail the abuses that Hester Dethridge suffers at her husband's hands. Refusing to work, Joel Dethridge spends all of Hester's small inheritance in drinking and enjoying himself. When she is forced to find a job to support them, his obnoxious behavior at the places where she works repeatedly gets her fired. He sells the furniture she has bought to get money to buy drink; he goes away and returns at will, always managing to trace her no matter where she has moved. And he beats her mercilessly, knocking out teeth and finally hitting her so hard that her ability to speak is impaired.

Hester does not suffer silently. She repeatedly seeks legal help to protect herself, but her quests are always useless. No mechanism exists, she is told, to keep her husband away from her if he chooses to stay: "If he had run off from me, something might have been done (as I understood) to protect me. But he stuck to his wife—as long as I could make a farthing he stuck to his wife. Being married to him I had no right to have left him; I was bound to go with my husband; there was no escape for me" (chap. 54, pt. 6). Nor can his legal right to her possessions be abridged. The only protection for her property could have been written into a premarital legal agreement, a provision Hester had not known about before she married and probably could not have afforded if she had.

Even more than the squalid living conditions and the physical danger to which Hester is exposed by her marriage, her emotional isolation is a major factor in her decision to kill. Unlike Palmer, for whom Frances Power Cobbe's advocacy secured a job which protected her from her husband, Hester Dethridge's appeals for help are rebuffed. Her family scorns her for marrying beneath her, and her clergyman is unable to cope with her anguish. While she earns the admiration and sympathy of her employers, none of them will tolerate the commotion that her husband's presence inevitably brings.

Moving constantly in a hopeless effort to forestall her husband's return, Hester lacks even the comfort that familiar surroundings and valued possessions can provide. She explains her dilemma this way:

> Where was the remedy? There was no remedy, but to try and escape him once more. Why didn't I have him locked up [for beating me]? What was the good of having him locked up? In a few weeks he would be out of the prison; sober and penitent, and promising amendment—and then when the fit took him, there he would be, the same furious savage that he had been often and often before. My heart got hard under the hopelessness of it; and dark thoughts began to beset me, mostly at night. About this time I began to say to myself, "There's no deliverance from this but in death—his death or mine. [chap. 54]

But she cannot kill herself. Her misery does not make her overwrought and excitable but cold and hard. She tortures herself by feeling that anyone else, given the same provocation, would have risen above the temptation she feels. In describing her resolution to kill, she comments: "Horrid—I am well aware this is horrid. Nobody else, in my place, would have ended as wickedly as that. All the other women in the world, tried as I was, would have risen superior to the trial" (chap. 54). In her resolution to kill him, she feels herself cut off from humanity and from forgiveness. But her desperation is so strong that she cannot stop herself.

Hester's compulsion distinguishes her from Lydia Gwilt, whose decision to murder was always a choice from which she maintained intellectual and even emotional distance. Dethridge, once committed to murder, hopes for outside forces to intervene but never wavers in her own determination. Concocting an elaborate plan, she manages to gain access to the room in which her drunken husband has locked himself and smothers him. The police conclude he died of natural causes brought about by acute alcoholism. Dethridge's guilty conscience and her dread of dis-

covery are complex emotions, and Collins wants the reader to
struggle with her culpability. She has committed a premeditated
murder to which she has not confessed. She feels no remorse,
but she is haunted by the memory of her crime. Not only does
she constantly punish herself with self-imposed silence and
isolation, but she is tortured by the recurrent vision of a spirit,
a specter of herself, urging her to kill again:

> I felt . . . a creeping chill come slowly over my flesh, and
> then a suspicion of something hidden near me, which would
> steal out and show itself if I looked that way. . . .
> The Thing stole out, dark and shadowy in the pleasant
> sunlight. At first I saw only the dim figure of a woman.
> After a little it began to get plainer, brightening from
> within outward—brightening, brightening, brightening,
> till it set before me the vision of MY OWN SELF, repeated
> as if I were standing before a glass—the double of myself
> looking at me with my own eyes . . . ; and it said to me,
> with my own voice, "Kill him." [chap. 54, pt. 14]

Collins leaves Hester's urge to murder open to interpretation.
Many of the novel's characters suspect she is insane. The medical
profession would, no doubt, have used menopause to explain her
visions and the resulting mania. The devout could point to the
repressed remnants of her orthodox Christianity, which would
condemn her for breaking the commandments no matter how
profound her provocation. But closest to Collins's own point is
that she cannot stop herself by force of will when confronted
with a scene which recalls so clearly her own miserable marriage.
Her second murder is not a random crime: she is an avenging
protectress, not a demonic force, for she kills Geoffrey Delamayn
at the moment he is about to murder his wife. Hester's urgency
to save Anne, with whom she feels kinship as an abused woman,
is compounded by her violent hatred of Delamayn, hatred based
in part on his disposition and in part on his knowledge of her
guilty past.

Although Anne is responsible to some extent for her unhappy
marriage by having forced Delamayn into a loveless union to
legitimize their child who was then born dead, the novel's

message is clear: men have no right to abuse their wives physically or psychologically. If they do, Collins warns, they will be destroyed either by the vengeance of a misused woman—like Dethridge—or by the poison of their own warped values—like Anne's father.

The consequences of the second murder complicate the novel's other point, that women must protect themselves and each other, for Anne's dramatic rescue is won at the expense of Hester's sanity. In each case Hester's motives are clear and her violent actions are not only justifiable but even beneficial. Had she not killed Joel Dethridge, sooner or later he would have killed her, and if she had not killed Geoffrey Delamayn, Anne would have been slain. Yet what the law and the reader might well excuse destroys Hester Dethridge: her mind is unhinged and she is institutionalized.

Collins wants it both ways. The novel brings the burning social issue of physical wife abuse to the public's attention without risking condemnation for letting a woman killer escape unpunished. In some ways, of course, mental oblivion may be the kindest resolution for a woman who cannot forgive herself for violence. But for a novelist who insisted that fiction had the right and responsibility to confront serious social issues head on and to treat women as responsible adults, it is disturbingly conventional. What, we are tempted to ask, kept him from having her not charged with murder on the basis of self-defense or having her tried and acquitted?

The novels after *Man and Wife* are neither as original nor as well-developed as those Collins wrote in the 1860s. As he became increasingly committed to the novel as a platform for social criticism, his work became cruder, and often more rigid and conventional, in its presentation of dangerous women. A typical example is his examination of obsessive mother-love in *Jezebel's Daughter* (1880). Yet some of the novels elaborate ideas raised earlier and hint at the direction that popular mystery fiction was headed in its treatment of women criminals: toward a greater complexity of motivation and an increasing urgency for self-protection.

The Legacy of Cain (1888) is the most interesting of the later books. Dominated by women, it sustains reader curiosity if not critical approval. Characteristically, Collins has a thesis to exploit as well as a story to tell; because the two are so closely intertwined, the result contributes several new ideas to his treatment of the criminal personality and the effects of heredity and environment on criminal behavior. The plot is dramatic, if contrived: two girls—Helena, the daughter of a clergyman, and Eunice, the daughter of a murderess—are brought up to believe they are really sisters. Since their home is not only comfortably middle class but also devoutly religious, and each girl is treated in exactly the same way, the narrator suggests that if one of them can be provoked to murder it will be the daughter of the criminal, not the daughter of the clergyman. Yet just the opposite happens. In fact, Helena Gracedieu is Collins's most cruel and vicious woman and the only one impervious to her own guilt.

The novel raises some provocative questions about the genesis of a woman's criminal behavior. If deprivation, abuse, passion, greed, or self-preservation does not provide the motive for crime, what does? In each of Collins's earlier works at least one of those factors was present. But Helena seems at first to act only for spite. On the other hand, she is intelligent and ambitious, bored with her housekeeping duties, and frustrated by her repressed sexuality. Nor is there any reason for her to think that the future holds the chance of much improvement. So while Collins intends her to be reprehensible, it is hard to ignore the roots of her malaise. Her situation is a variation on Lydia Gwilt's.

The attempted murder, though, is blatant enough to eliminate any sympathy for her. She does not love the man she tries to kill although they are engaged, and there is nothing to be gained financially whether she marries him or not. He has not abused her, although he does not love her; she is more self-reliant than he is and perfectly capable of getting along without him. But the fact that he is not enthralled with her annoys her, and so she poisons him. At least that way she can be sure he will not marry her sister, of whom she is jealous.

The inescapable conclusion is that she is a vicious human

being. The narrator observes, in analyzing Helena's "diabolical depravity," "the doctrine of hereditary transmission of moral qualities must own that it has overlooked the fertility (for growth of good and for growth of evil equally) which is inherent in human nature. There are virtues that exalt us, and vices that degrade us, whose mysterious origin is, not in our parents, but in ourselves" (Postscript). Helena feels no remorse, and apparently no shame for attempted murder. After serving her sentence, she moves to America and becomes an outspoken, even passionate and extremely popular advocate of women's rights.

Collins had been building up to such an ending during his entire career as a novelist. Minor characters in earlier books survived their criminal acts unscathed. Heroines accused of moral, but not criminal, deviance pursued and won their right to happiness. But never before had a woman guilty of violent crime been impervious to social disgrace and her own conscience. Helena is not admirable, but she is aggressive and yet womanly; she explodes the persistent Victorian cliché that criminal women were inevitably doomed because they had denied their essential womanhood. She never considers suicide and certainly does not become insane. And the narrator, pressed to say that she will pay for her crimes, dismisses the likelihood of the "poetical justice" she deserves with a scornful "poetical fiddlesticks!" (chap. 62).

Collins, exploring subjects and developing characters unimagined before, is explicit about the complexity of women's emotions, their cultural oppression, and their sexual passions. Yet sometimes he faults women for being manipulative, much as he criticizes men for their inhumanity to women. The effect is to emphasize the similarity, rather than the difference, of sexual exploitation and criminal motivation in both genders. His candor and zeal in assaulting the self-satisfied hypocrisy of the Victorian bourgeoisie and the oppressive respectability of the novelists who wrote for them produced radical changes in the way criminal women were conceived in the fiction that followed.

But it would be wrong to suggest that Collins transcended his era. The novelist's work is full of conflicts between radicalism and orthodoxy which leave the reader ultimately uncertain about his views. For example, in *Man and Wife*, his most outspoken assault on male privilege, he seems torn between deploring the anti-woman bias which allowed society to ignore, if not condone, wife abuse, and advocating the view that women's "natural condition" was to be dependent on men. Similarly, he stresses women's capacity to commit crimes for self-aggrandizement and their need to commit crimes in self-defense, but until his last novel he never lets a woman escape punishment. He was willing to show women shaking their collective fist at society, but he was not ready to let them break down its gender barriers.

SEVEN

Thomas Hardy:
A Desperate Remedy

Dickens and Eliot portrayed their women criminals (and would-be criminals) as complex characters. They touched, sometimes very delicately, on the questions that female criminality posed in mid-Victorian England: how could a true woman kill and how was she to be judged? The sensation writers like Braddon and Collins added bizarre touches—murder victims thrown down wells and suspected killers imprisoned in insane asylums—but emphasized the link between physical and psychological abuse in a woman's decision to murder. By 1889, Thomas Hardy was prepared to develop the character of the Victorian woman criminal—in the person of Tess Durbeyfield—to its most compelling potential.

Despite Tess's murder of Alec d'Urberville and her cruel punishment, Hardy insists she is a "pure woman." He means that she is pure sexually, despite her illegitimate child and her renewed liaison with Alec. But more important, she is a pure woman because she is completely and totally womanly. Her faults, like the touch of imperfection Angel sees in her otherwise perfect lips and her quick temper, make her more appealing because they make her more human, more alive.

For what can she be blamed, before the murder? For too much innocence? For too much honesty? For a temper that flares when she is tormented by a man whose motives she has every reason to despise? In this, she is unlike Dickens's and Eliot's women criminals, who are rarely endearing even when they are sympathetic. They represent those traits which stereotype intolerable women: DeFarge's aggressiveness, Hortense's irrationality and deceit, Hetty and Gwendolen's self-absorption and social ambitions. Tess shares none of these. If anything, she surpasses the conventional woman in looks, intelligence, and charm. But because she is working-class and can be labeled as promiscuous, she pays with her life for breaking the law.

Although Tess is guilty of the murder for which she is hanged, Hardy insists that she is unjustly punished. The problem Hardy tackles with Tess, whose execution is also intolerable to the reader, is the most provocative involving criminals of either sex: the tension created by sympathetic characters who are guilty of crime. Because it is impossible for a novelist—or a reader— to condemn such men or women after exploring their motives and examining their justifications, guilt is often ignored, or even excused, despite moral, ethical, or legal considerations. Dostoyevsky's Rodion Raskolnikov is an example of such a character. Other novelists, such as Victor Hugo in *Les Miserables*, draw sympathetic characters who endure unjust punishments to underline social criticism and encourage changes in the law. For Hardy, the issue was the inequitable social and judicial treatment based on class and gender.

The tension between Tess's provocation to kill and the violent murder she commits takes on an added political dimension: the question of women's rights. Her story typifies the plight of physically and psychologically battered women who turn to violence as a last resort. Her violence is engendered by the actions of Alec d'Urberville, from the rape at the beginning to its economic and emotional consquences. While other events contribute to Tess's destruction, none overshadows the avenging power of an abused woman. She kills Alec because he has destroyed her chance for happiness, not once but over and over. Ironically her liberating act dooms her to hang: the abused woman and the killer are inextricably bound together in her tragedy.

In recent years women who have murdered battering husbands, fathers, or lovers have frequently been applauded for striking a blow for equality and justice. This has been especially true when they acted in self-defense, or in what they *perceived* to be self-defense. Sometimes they have been acquitted despite clear evidence against them because their victim had so clearly provoked the assault. A *New Yorker* cartoon (26 March 1984) epitomizes the point: a woman, sitting in front of a television set, reassures the curious man behind her, "You missed the end, but it came out happily. She shot him." For Hardy and his Victorian audience, women's demands for equality and autonomy were not so explicit—and controversial—an endorsement of violence. But *Tess of the d'Urbervilles* makes clear that Hardy did not think of his protagonist as a criminal. He portrays her death as a travesty of justice.

The story of a girl seduced was common enough.[1] On 1 January 1892, writing about *Tess*, Hardy commented: "As to my choice of such a character after such a fall, it has been borne in upon my mind for many years that justice has never been done to such women in fiction. I do not know if the rule is general, but in this country the girls who have made the mistake of Tess almost invariably lead chaste lives thereafter, even under strong temptation."[2]

There is no evidence to either prove or disprove Hardy's contention that most girls make only one mistake. But in *Tess*, Hardy is not primarily an observer of general social mores; he is the architect of a catastrophe. Neither her husband Angel Clare nor her own sense of responsibility allows Tess to put her past behind her. Her second fall is a matter of economic necessity—as it was for so many poor women. Her temptation is not sexual; she is not "tempted by a dream of happiness." She relents grimly and gives in to Alec's importuning to become his mistress almost five years after their initial, brief relationship because it seems to her—in her desperate financial situation—the only way to provide security for her mother and siblings.

Accepting this motive is critical to understanding Hardy's novel. The hopelessness of her family plight and the degree to which she blames herself for their eviction from Marlott make her vulnerable. Earlier, when the family horse was killed in a road accident, Tess felt compelled to seek assistance from the nouveau riche family that had adopted the d'Urberville name. This time, faced with the insurmountable task of providing food and shelter for her family, Tess finally accepts Alec's persistent offer of aid at the price of sexual acquiescence. In each case, her father, theoretically the family's provider, fails her. First his drunken negligence and then his untimely death force her to assume a provider's role which she is unprepared to fill. Her husband fails her as well, through his moral rigidity. And her mother, unable to make any contribution of her own to the family's financial needs, urges Tess both times to capitalize on the d'Urberville connection. It is unreliable maternal advice if there ever was any.

Some critics have argued that Tess prostitutes herself in returning to Alec and is thus self-destructive and culpable even if Hardy did not want her to seem so.[3] Others, like Evelyn Hardy, assert that Tess is the victim of her own sexuality, so determined to suffer that she deliberately seeks masochistic relationships. Such interpretations are not consistent with the text. Worse, they grow out of the discredited practice of blaming abused women—indeed any victims—for inviting their own misery.[4]

These arguments ignore the options (or, more accurately, the lack of options) which Hardy allows Tess in his depiction of rural Victorian society. Hardy's realism—though often overlaid with symbol and legend—clearly conveys the effect of class distinctions on human behavior, especially women's behavior. Poor unmarried women who were not in domestic service had the choice of uncertain employment at agricultural labor (like Iz and Marion) or moving to industrialized urban centers where they frequently were forced into prostitution in order to survive.[5] Unlike Sue Bridehead (in *Jude the Obscure*), who might have found work as a schoolmistress, or Bathsheba Everdene (in *Far from the Madding Crowd*), who owned a farm, Tess had few choices of employment, and none of them provided the means to support Joan Durbeyfield and her children. Her consistent refusal to ask for or accept favors can be seen as a sign of excessive pride only if one thinks the poor have no right to be proud.

The inescapable correlative of her decision to live with Alec is her belief that Angel has abandoned her forever because she is a compromised woman. In the face of that rejection, she no longer cares what happens to her. Hardy offers the passivity, the ennui, which characterizes her in the parlor of the Sandbourne lodging house as a horrifying contrast to her behavior earlier in the text when her will to live could always triumph over depression, defeat, and even the urge to commit suicide. But living with Alec provides financial security for her family; suicide would have left them to starve. Until the moment of Angel's return, that recognition controls her revulsion and her passionate hatred.

But Tess's is more than the story of a depressed woman or a pragmatic one. Until the moment she strikes Alec with the carving knife, hers might be the story of any woman's disgrace. But when Tess acts, she pulls herself out of the traditional pattern of the female victim and becomes an assertive woman. Because she must pay with her life, she becomes a tragic figure.

A contemporary event, the trial of Florence Maybrick for killing her husband, provides some of the background for Hardy's conception of Tess's motives. In August 1889, immediately after Maybrick's conviction and during the period Hardy was deeply involved in writing *Tess*, he observed: "When a married woman who has a lover kills her husband, she does not really wish to kill the husband; she wishes to kill the situation. Of course in Clytemnestra's case it was not exactly so, since there was the added grievance of Iphigenia, which half-justified her."[6] Hardy's implicit association of Tess's tragedy with Florence Maybrick's trial and conviction affirms the importance of sexual behavior in assessing a woman's guilt and the significance of social class in determining the judgment that will be executed against her. At the same time, his allusion to Clytemnestra evokes not only the tragic proportions of Tess's story but also the subject of "true marriage," the au courant topic of the last decades of the nineteenth century.

Despite the obvious differences between Maybrick's story and Tess's, the underlying issues are astoundingly similar: a woman's subservient role in marriage or a marriage-like relationship, the blame borne by a woman guilty of sexual misconduct, and the outraged official response to a woman's violence even when it is directed against an abusive husband. In some ways the governing issue in the Maybrick trial was extramarital sex.[7] Florence Maybrick had been married for seven years to a cotton merchant several years older than she when he died unexpectedly. Of all the complicated facets of the case, the most germane—and sensational—appeared to be her brief adulterous relationship with a young man named Brierly.[8]

In his charge to the grand jury investigating the case in July 1889, Mr. Justice Stephen said: "I hardly know how to put it otherwise than this: that if a woman does carry on an adulterous intrigue with another man, it may supply every sort of motive . . . why she should wish to get rid of her husband."[9] Stephen's obsession with Florence Maybrick's adultery and its potential influence on her motive to kill her husband are rampant in the record of the trial itself, particularly in his summary statement:

> You must remember the intrigue which she carried on with this man Brierly, and the feelings—it seems horrible to comparatively ordinary innocent people—a horrible and incredible thought that a woman should be plotting the death of her husband in order that she might be left at liberty to follow her own degrading vices. . . . There is no doubt that the propensities which lead persons to vices of that kind kill all the more tender, all the more manly, or all the more womanly feelings of the human mind. . . . I will not say anything about it, except that it is easy enough to conceive how a horrible woman, in so terrible a position, might be assailed by some fearful and terrible temptation.[10]

His view clearly carried the day, for the jury deliberated only thirty-five minutes before pronouncing her guilty, although the conflicting medical evidence left in doubt whether he had been poisoned or not. Florence Maybrick was condemned for murder but was held equally reprehensible for adultery in the eyes of the judge and jury. Stephen sentenced her to hang.[11]

Despite the fact that such devastating use was made of Maybrick's brief extramarital affair, no evidence of her husband's infidelities was introduced into the proceedings. Yet he had kept a mistress, supporting her and her children, during the entire course of his marriage. Indeed, when Mrs. Maybrick initiated her well-grounded but abortive effort to win a divorce, her husband threatened her with total separation from her children on the grounds that she was an unfit mother, despite the fact that adultery would have been proved against him, not her, as a condition of the divorce. It is a curious parallel that the argument which persuades Tess that Angel is right about separating from her is his outrageous (to modern ears) assertion that whatever children their marriage *might* produce *might* someday hear the story of their mother's shame and be shamed themselves and alienated from her (chap. 36). Recent scholarship has shown that despite the increasing willingness to hold men accountable both for extramarital affairs and for other behavior formerly excused as "understandably typically masculine," in practical terms blame still fell on women to an appalling degree.

Hardy, we know, was deeply concerned with the subject of marriage and the effects of married life on man and wife. The marriages in his earlier novels are punctuated with violence: sword-play, guns, man-traps, drowning. If, as others have argued, *Tess* is the synthesis of Hardy's ideas on marriage, that is especially true about marriage's potential violence, both physical and psychological.[12]

One of the haunting questions of the novel is the nature of Tess's wifehood. Legally and spiritually—and at long last physically—she is Angel Clare's wife. Their fleeting reunion and consummation in the face of certain catastrophe is the romantic culmination of their love story. But Tess's earlier union with Alec mars her true marriage and confuses her own values. Her return to d'Urberville is partially explained—albeit unsatisfactorily for many readers—by her conviction that d'Urberville is her real husband. In an age when premarital relationships are commonplace, Tess's belief "that in a physical sense [Alec] alone was her husband" (chap. 51) may seem quaint to some. To others, it is further evidence of Tess's willful self-defeat. But

Tess is profoundly conscious of the values of her own age; for her, sexual union with Alec, their mutual child, and his role as provider (which I have already discussed) make him her husband in fact if not in law.

Compounding her confusion is the powerlessness of their legal union to force Angel Clare to be her husband. He does not sleep with her, nor does he provide for her. Indeed, he tells Tess that it is Alec—and not he—who is her "husband in nature" (chap. 36), and he insists that he and Tess cannot live as man and wife while Alec is alive. Similarly, d'Urberville affirms the idea that Tess should be married to him. As soon as he discovers that he has fathered her child, he comes to Hintcomb-Ash "to make the only reparation I can make for the trick I played on you: that is, will you be my wife?" (chap. 46). When she will not, he insists it would be "morally right and proper" for them to marry. Her legal marriage to Angel does not interfere with Alec's physical desire for her or prevent his persistent and ultimately successful efforts to win her back.

While she rejects his advances, she is fleetingly tempted to accept him once before her family's expulsion from their home makes her desperate. Her motive is financial then too: "She did for one moment picture what might have been the result if she had been free to accept the offer just made her of being the *monied* Alec's wife. It would have lifted her completely out of subjection, not only to her present oppressive employer, but to a whole world who seemed to despise her" (chap. 46, my italics). Financial security, after all, was for many Victorian women the most persuasive reason to marry.

The two husbands (and non-husbands) represent the ways Tess is abused as a woman and as a wife. In the most traditional way, Alec the libertine master takes sexual advantage not only of her innocence but of her position as serving girl in his household. Later, Angel rejects her when she does not conform to the image of a perfect, pure woman that his culture demands. Because she does not demand her rights—indeed is in no position to know that she has rights—these men hold the power to manipulate her life.

Tess's characteristic reaction to these catastrophes of being

Tess as supplicant rather than avenger dominated the illustrations for the serialized version of *Tess of the d'Urbervilles*, part of an editorial effort to mask Hardy's most powerful moments. Illustration by E. Borough Johnson for the *Graphic*, 1891. General Research Division, the New York Public Library, Astor, Lenox, and Tilden Foundations.

a woman—her pregnancy, Angel's rejection, and her final yield-
ing to d'Urberville—is passivity—that feminine virtue so widely
admired in ideal Victorian women. In each case what she dreads
most happens, yet she makes no effort to fight her situation or
turn it to her advantage. Indeed, her depression at the first
disaster turns suicidal at the second and third. When Angel
finds her at Sandbourne, she is so changed, so passive it seems
to him "that his original Tess had spiritually ceased to recognize
the body before him as hers—allowing it to drift, like a corpse
upon the current, in a direction disassociated from its living
will" (chap. 55).

Her sense of herself is as unforgiven and unforgivable, but
it changes after she kills Alec, a new death sentence replacing
the old. With Alec dead, she and Angel are able to resume their
interrupted marriage. But even then she fears his love cannot
last. Despite the bliss in which they pass their long-delayed
honeymoon, she senses that the murder dooms her to be despised; Tess makes no effort to escape (rejecting Angel's half-
hearted attempts to flee) and no effort to resist arrest. And when
Angel is not sure that they will be reunited after death, her
response is resigned and passive. She objects, but she does not
put up a fight.

This passivity, a curious adjunct to her violence, masks the
turmoil of her inner rebellion. It is first evident in her agreeing
to seek out the d'Urbervilles after the death of the family horse;
it recurs when she rejects Alec after discovering her pregnancy;
and it lasts, with one bitter exception in her confrontation with
the minister who will not bury her child, until she leaves for
her new start at Talbothays.

Because her child is born during this period of passivity,
Hardy paints a curious picture of Tess as parent. Mothering
was highly valued in Victorian England as a woman's most
critical contribution to the family and to the society at large.
"Unnatural" mothers were despised and suspected of perverse
crimes. Yet significantly Hardy shows Tess as one who never
quite masters her role as mother. It is all the more curious
because she is so wonderful a sister (and surrogate parent) to
her many younger siblings. Her ambivalence toward her own

unwanted motherhood is caused, the novelist tells us, by the attitudes of conventional society which had permeated her own consciousness and made this child of shame hard for her to love. But at the crisis of Sorrow's young life, as the child is about to die, Tess's passion rises to the surface and she begs God for its life.

Her response to Sorrow, more than any other single event, defines the unique nature of her ultimate violence against Alec. For infanticide, not the murder of adults, was the classic woman's crime of the era. Yet Tess, despite her estrangement from the baby, never thinks of killing it although she speaks often of her own death. When she at last kills Alec, she strikes against injustice and untruth, against abuse and manipulation. While she claims she was "wickedly mad" to murder, many readers see a more human, and more justifiable, rationality in her action.

For if Tess has tortured herself about her loss of maidenhood and the loss of Angel, her greatest humiliation is her return to Alec. "You have torn my life all to pieces . . . made me be what I prayed you in pity not to make me again!" she cries to Alec after she leaves Angel standing, bewildered, in the Sandbourne dining room.[13] It is the penultimate price she pays for her rape, the one which robs her of her personality and—as far as she is concerned—her dignity. But Hardy assaults the facade of late Victorian society by casting this mistress as vulnerable and sympathetic rather than as a whore or a blight.

Her final payment, execution for Alec's murder, is barely discussed in the novel. It is an omission for which Hardy has been both vehemently criticized and warmly praised. There is no court-room scene: we do not see Tess in the prisoner's box or hear the prosecution's case. But can we doubt that the history of her illegitimate child and her adultery were used against her?

True, she is hanged in part because she excites no particular political or social sympathy; she has no friends in high places. But the most compelling reason—as the actual criminal cases suggest—is her class and her gender. What better evidence does the jury need than her compromised morality? If she has already broken the seventh commandment, why would she hesitate to break the sixth as well?[14]

Tess, from the first, uses physical violence against Alec in a way that she does against no one else. In repeated scenes, from their first meeting until their last, she is roused to anger and responds with pushing, slapping, and finally stabbing. Indeed, when she chooses a knife for the murder, the novelist emphasizes her violence, and the assertive energy (or rage) needed to stab a man to death. As Simon Gatrell points out in the comprehensive introduction to the Grindle-Gatrell edition of *Tess*, the revisions on the characterization of his heroine that Hardy made in the 1889 manuscript before publication stress Tess's anger and independence in the scenes with Alec. At the same time greater attention focuses on Alec's manipulative, even evil, qualities. Gatrell suggests, too, that Tess blushes more in the text version than in the earlier manuscript "to show her more aggressively responsive to emotional pressure—occasionally sexual, but often due to embarrassment or anger."[15]

That part of her character capable of committing murder is frequently visible and totally believable throughout the novel. On the fateful evening in the Chase when Alec rapes her, she nearly pushes him from his horse even before he begins to make sexual advances. When, shortly after, she runs away from Trantridge, she threatens to push him out of his gig when he questions the sincerity of her claims of innocence. The violence he arouses in her, akin perhaps to the passion which she feels in a positive way toward Angel Clare, is revealed most powerfully when she violently slaps Alec across the mouth with her leather glove at threshing time, and later when she slams the casement window on his arm when he follows her home.

This potential for violent action, which is otherwise dormant, reveals itself fleetingly in the moments when Tess describes her attempt to kill herself after Angel rejects her. But she has a peculiar view of suicide, one bound up with her belief in punishment. She insists that Angel really ought to kill her, for she has ruined his expectations and offered him no way to get out of the marriage. This incident anticipates her murder of Alec; she does exactly what she said Angel ought to do: kill the person who had ruined his hopes and dreams.

Tess also senses in herself not only the capacity but the desire to kill. As she tells Angel when she confesses the murder: "I owed it to you, and to myself, Angel. I feared long ago, when I struck him on the mouth with my glove, that I might do it some day for the trap he set for me in my simple youth, and his wrong to you through me" (chap. 57). In her eyes, it was her *obligation* to kill, as it had been her obligation to make up for the loss of the horse, to tell Angel the truth about herself, to resist writing against his orders, and to go back to Alec after he bailed out her family.

There is more to her revenge, too. While Alec does not abuse her physically after the rape, he does torment her relentlessly. Like the satanic character he is, he hounds her about her two greatest vulnerabilities: her sexual appeal and her husband's absence. She reacts toward him as a woman does toward an intolerable and abusive husband. Her crime is domestic and sexual, in the best tradition of Victorian criminal cases with women defendants and of Victorian novels. In this sense, Tess like Gwendolen Harleth and perhaps Florence Maybrick, is repaying abuse with the only sure revenge—death. It is no coincidence that these comparisons are cases in which husbands die. For the idea Hardy introduces from the moment of Tess's brief return to Marlott after her gruelling year of separation from Angel—that Alec really is her husband—is borne out in her violence.

While Michael Millgate is right in claiming that Hardy does not justify or glorify the murder, for some readers, the murder scene is disappointing; it often seems that those who most vehemently accuse Hardy of sensationalism are those most disappointed that the gory details are missing.[16] Realistically, of course, it lacks the dramatic power of comparable moments in *Agamemnon* or *The Duchess of Malfi*, two works that have been cited as sources for *Tess*. Conversely, the blood dripping through the floor boards to the ceiling below and providing the first hint of crime smacks of the incredible. Yet the event which clearly inspired that detail occurred at Dartmoor in 1888, suggesting that sensationalism is possible in life as well as art.[17] Perhaps the greatest tampering with reality that Hardy does is to make Tess murder with a knife rather than the customary woman's weapon—arsenic. On the other hand, poetic justice makes the knife through the heart seem exactly the right death for Alec.

Unlike Nina Auerbach, who describes Tess's murder of Alec and her execution as being "Hardy's final conformity to Victorian conventions" because "the execution of a killer was not yet revolting to society's liberal guilts and fears,"[18] I suggest that Hardy made the execution a part of his novel in order to lodge an outraged protest against the treatment of women—especially poor, "fallen" women—by society in general and the courts in particular. The mystery which shrouds Tess from the time she is arrested at Stonehenge blunts the sense that the reader has of her as a criminal and overlays her story with an aura of primeval sacrifice that confronts the realism of Tess's punishment as the verdict of an implacable and biased system of justice.

For many readers, Hardy falters in the final chapters of the novel, losing not only the dramatic intensity so carefully built up through the Durbeyfields' displacement from Marlott, but even the realism necessary to make the murder and its aftermath believable. Perhaps the publisher's critical reaction to the novel which admittedly influenced some of Hardy's prepublication revisions made him hesitant to treat so incendiary a subject. But for me the vacuum of inhumanity into which Tess vanishes after her arrest makes Hardy's protest at her fate as lucid as a blow-by-blow account of the trial and execution would have done.[19]

Some critics have claimed that Hardy is not particularly interested in the implications of her crime, either for Tess or for her society, but is more concerned with the tragedy of her destruction. Without doubt, Tess's action is the culmination of five years of pain and a year and a half of bitter hatred. Sparked by Angel's return, something that Tess has given up hoping for, and fed by Alec's mockery, her self-control explodes into violence. Hers is not a premeditated act but a spontaneous one. But it does not lack motives.

Tess's own explanations are confused, for she quickly recognizes the consequences of Alec's death: she can have Angel. Her obligation to kill Alec for his transgressions becomes the opportunity to get Angel back. Her recognition of that relationship "came . . . as a shining light" only after the deed, and is consistent with the idea that the murder is a spontaneous act of outrage. But she must know—subconsciously—from the moment Angel returns that Alec will have to die if she is to be reunited with her husband.

In this instance, more than any other, Tess's revolutionary womanhood asserts itself. Unable to depend on anyone else before, and forced to act alone, she does so again. If Alec is going to die, she will have to kill him. And, briefly, she succeeds in altering her world. After the murder, however, she is unable to act or to plan; once more she becomes passive. She is content in the brief moment of bliss that her violence has bought. In fact, as she tells Angel, she has no expectations for the future, preferring death to the knowledge that he despises her—as she is sure he will.

Has Tess lost her instinct for self-preservation? Is her ultimate surrender, without struggle, her long-desired suicide, the appropriate recognition of guilt that becomes a murderer? Or has Hardy played false with Tess, undercutting her love for life with his urgency to make her sympathetic? As long as Tess is a victim, pity is possible. But if she is not only dangerous but also resourceful and clever, how can she also be a classic Victorian heroine? Caught in the very system of values he is exposing, Hardy makes Tess give up the fight.

Ironically, Angel can forgive murder, although he could not forgive Tess's sexual experience. Earlier tolerance would have prevented the later tragedy. That he is quick to accept her love for him as the motive for murder demeans; so does his willingness to blame mental imbalance or the legend of the d'Urberville coach for her action. No one, not even her beloved Angel, can see the murder as the inevitable consequence of Alec's own behavior toward Tess and as the only solution to Tess's intolerable situation.

Tess, in this scheme of things, must die on the scaffold because she has no remorse for her crime. She is not sorry Alec is dead and she does not regret killing him. Her highly developed sense of fatalism and her recognition that everyone must pay society's dues make her own fate clear to her. She is more dangerous to the idea of Victorian morality than most readers are willing to acknowledge, for she lives by a different standard than that society was willing to allow.

EIGHT

Arthur Conan Doyle:
Vengeance Is Hers

At the very end of the Victorian era, Sir Arthur Conan Doyle
wrote crime fiction that made his detective Sherlock Holmes a
protagonist par excellence. The women in Doyle's Holmes stories
are generally dismissed as trivial, no match for the detective or
Dr. Watson. True, many of them are ciphers, pale ladies who
need to be rescued by clever, strong men from the abusive
behavior of other men or the rigidity of social custom. In those
cases, Holmes prefers, as he comments in "A Case of Identity"
(1891), "to do business with the male relatives." But other Doyle
women are highly assertive and sometimes nefarious characters;
in fact, more than twenty women in the Holmes stories can
quite legitimately be described as active criminals. They are
implicated in murder, blackmail, robbery, assault, and criminal
collusion from the earliest stories until the end of Doyle's career.
In *The Sign of the Four* (1890), for example, Holmes makes the
perverse remark that "the most winning woman I ever knew
was hanged for poisoning three little children for their insurance-
money" (chap. 2). The reader can only conclude that this unnamed culprit was much more vibrant (before her hanging, of
course) than the sweet and essentially insipid ladies admired by
Watson.

Janus-like, Doyle incorporated comments about deviant women typical of the century just ending into his stories while
anticipating the new attitudes toward criminality that would

flourish in twentieth-century crime fiction. For example, when his women murder or are suspected of murder, the taint of infidelity or sexual indiscretion is always involved, putting Doyle firmly in the mainstream of Victorian attitudes about the moral behavior of criminal women. But Doyle rejects the conventional view that "sin" explains why a woman robs or murders and attributes as much complexity and determination to his criminal women as he does to comparable male characters. While sometimes women act as they do because of the influence of strong criminal men, equally often they act alone, motivated by vengeance, greed, or desperation. Invariably those crimes a woman commits independently, especially crimes of violence, are engendered by the betrayal or abuse of an unfaithful or unscrupulous man.

The reader suspects, for instance, that Irene Adler in "A Scandal in Bohemia" (1891) would never have threatened blackmail if her lover had not deserted her for a more suitable, upper-class wife. Nor did her sexual liaison with the King rule out her own quite respectable and apparently happy marriage to a London lawyer. Watson may think she is "of dubious and questionable memory," but neither Holmes nor the reader shares his view. Although she is not a violent woman, Adler's sexual liberation, her extraordinary cleverness and daring, characterize Doyle's most interesting women. She has a "soul of steel" and "the face of the most beautiful of women and the mind of the most resolute of men." Yet Adler's mental acumen and cunning do not make her masculine. Watson makes it clear, for example, that Holmes was beaten by a "woman's wit," and Holmes himself describes Adler as "a lovely woman, with a face a man might die for." Doyle wanted his readers to appreciate his brilliant, ruthless, successful, *womanly* antagonist.

The implicit theme of "A Scandal in Bohemia"—the extent to which public scandal and social destruction ride on sexual indiscretion—is explicit in "The Adventure of Charles Augustus Milverton" (1904). Women are the customary victims of the blackmailer Milverton's greed and ruthlessness, Sherlock Holmes asserts, because the social conventions forbid even the *appearance* of sexual indiscretion in the life of a respectable Victorian woman. Milverton has managed to avoid arrest because none of his victims has been bold enough to expose him and bear the public shame. Clearly, if justice is to be done, it must be done outside the law. And who is a more apt agent of vengeance than a wronged woman?

Holmes and Watson are witnesses to Milverton's execution because they have been hired by yet another of Milverton's intended victims to retrieve some incriminating materials from his safe. Once again Holmes's plan is bested by the cleverness and courage of a woman, but she has not come for incriminating material. That has already been delivered and her husband has died of shock. Instead, she has duped Milverton into a late-night rendezvous in order to kill him.

Her rage is explicit: "You will ruin no more lives as you ruined mine. You will wring no more hearts as you wrung mine. I will free the world of a poisonous thing. Take that, you hound, and that!—and that!—and that!—and that!" Nor is her clearly articulated rage calmed by shooting him full of bullets. "The woman looked at him intently and ground her heel into his upturned face. She looked again, but there was no sound or movement. I heard a sharp rustle, the night air blew into the heated room, and the avenger was gone."

The determination, cool-headedness, and brutality of Milverton's killer draws no direct comment from Holmes, but he makes two revealing decisions. He destroys all of the material in the safe and the note arranging the late-night meeting, thus leaving no clues as to the murderer's identity; and he refuses to assist in the police investigation. There can be no doubt his sympathy rests with the killer.

Yet the detective cannot rest until he has identified for himself the mysterious woman, who turns out to be the widow of a statesman and nobleman "with a time-honored title." How is this violent aristocrat, whose unelaborated indiscretions destroyed her husband and drove her to murder, related to Irene Adler? Beyond their rather exotic beauty and provocative sexuality, they share a sense of feminist rage and the personal courage to act on that rage.[1] Neither is deterred by feminine reticence or attempts at intimidation; neither is defeated by a reputedly clever adversary. Indeed, the fact that the Dark Lady does not accede to Milverton's demands, although she could easily have raised the blackmail money, suggests that she welcomes confrontation.

By making Adler's and the Dark Lady's crimes sympathetic, even admirable, Doyle defies the convention that women's criminality is not normal, just as he negates the assumption that the women's sexual experience brands them as immoral. But as Catherine Belsey points out in one of the few serious assessments of the Milverton tale, Doyle is silent about the sexual details which create so much havoc. "These stories," she says, "whose overt project is total explicitness, total verisimilitude in the interests of a plea for scientificity, are haunted by shadowy, mysterious amd often silent women."[2] Doyle goes further than other Victorian writers in dispelling the myths shrouding female criminality. His women are not abnormal or unbalanced. There is no suggestion that the Dark Lady will suffer psychological anguish—like Lady Macbeth or Gwendolen Harleth—for her crime. But he does require that readers imagine for themselves the circumstances which made her vulnerable to blackmail in the first place and that they accept the legitimacy of her husband's shocked reaction.

This disparity between candor and reticience is similarly evident in other stories which develop the theme of the dangerous woman. Kitty Winter, in the "Adventure of the Illustrious Client" (1925), threatens the life of Baron Adelbert Gruner, one of the "worst men in London." She, the most recent of Gruner's mistresses, is "so worn with sin and sorrow that one read the terrible years which had left their leprous mark upon her." The intensity of her hatred, such "as women seldom and men never can attain," is reminiscent of the searing emotions Dickens describes in the women of the French Revolution.

The deserted, nearly hysterical Winter insists on revenge. "I am not out for money," she exclaims, as Holmes tries to redirect her anger. "Let me see this man in the mud, and I've got all I worked for—in the mud *with my foot on his cursed face"* (my italics). Instead, she throws vitriol at him, ruining his good looks. For Winter, as for the Dark Lady earlier, personal violence is the only suitable revenge for arrogant, chauvinist abuse. It is a view Doyle makes the court endorse, for when Kitty Winter is tried for assault she receives the lowest sentence possible. Of course if Winter had been a lady, or even comfortably middle class, she might have escaped the judicial system altogether, but the point Doyle is making is that any system which gives men seemingly limitless power over women invites women's revolt.

At least eight other women commit murder or are suspected of it in the Holmes stories, all of them in connection with destructive marriages or romances. Some are mistresses, some betrayed wives, and some unfaithful wives; all but one kill or are accused of killing the man responsible for their unhappiness. Interestingly enough, none of them is ever punished by the courts, although several of the innocent ones are interviewed by the police, and Grace Dunbar, in "The Adventure of Thor Bridge" (1922), is committed for trial until Holmes uncovers the scheme by which she has been framed by her employer's jealous wife. Madness and suicide are sometimes the consequences of their violence, preceded in several instances by that favorite Victorian lady's malady, brain fever. Doyle, when he uses these extra-judicial punishments, is staunchly conventional, not much more willing than the majority of Victorian novelists to allow women to benefit from crime unscathed.

Yet he has Holmes, from the earliest stories, express a certain fascination with and sympathy for the women who have been caught up in unhappy love affairs, wronged by their husbands or lovers, or put into sexual danger.[3] The reader gets an insight into the detective's perception of what drives a woman to commit a violent crime when he comments in "The Musgrave Ritual" (1893): "What smouldering fire of vengeance had suddenly sprung into flame in this passionate Celtic woman's soul when she saw the man who had wronged her—wronged her perhaps far more than we suspect—in her power? Was it a chance that

The woman prisoner, though at the center of Gilbert's illustration
for "The Problem of Thor Bridge," is overshadowed by the powerful
presence of Sherlock Holmes, just as women—guilty or innocent—
were throughout the canon. *Strand Magazine*, 1922. General Research Division, the New York Public Library, Astor, Lenox, and
Tilden Foundations.

the wood had slipped . . . ? Had she only been guilty of silence . . . ? Or had some sudden blow from her hand dashed the support away and sent the slab crashing down into its place?" Holmes does not know the real story of the butler Brunton's entombment beneath the cellar floor of Hurlstone, of course, any more than the reader does, but he makes Rachel Howells's guilty responsibility entirely plausible. The woman's behavior after Brunton's disappearance, "her blanched face, her shaken nerves, her peals of hysterical laughter" are, according to Holmes, the typical reaction of a woman who must face the consequences of her own violent behavior.

This observation about the effects of crime on women echoes the words of other nineteenth-century writers. Dickens, for instance, says much the same thing of Lady Dedlock's reaction to Tulkinghorn's death in *Bleak House*, even though she does not actually kill him: "For, as her murderous perspective, before the doing of the deed, however subtle the precautions for its commission, would have been closed up by a gigantic dilatation of the hateful figure, preventing her from seeing any consequences beyond it; and as those consequences would have rushed in, in an unimagined flood, the moment the figure was laid low— which always happens when a murder is done; . . . The complications of her shame, her dread, remorse, and misery, overwhelms her at its height; and even her strength of self-reliance is overturned and whirled away, like a leaf before a mighty wind" (chap. 55). Doyle's conclusion, however, is very different from Dickens's. Lady Dedlock commits suicide, but Holmes imagines that Howells has gotten away "and carried herself, and the memory of her crime, to some land beyond the seas." True, she may not profit from murder, but she is not destroyed either.

Doyle's most explicit discussion of domestic violence as a motive for murder occurs in "The Adventure of the Abbey Grange" (1904), a story contemporaneous with "Charles Augustus Milverton." Lady Mary, the Australian-born wife of Sir Eustace Brackenstall, openly rebels against the rigidity of English marriage laws which have kept her tied to a drunken husband, and she tries valiantly (and successfully to everyone but Holmes) to cover up the truth of her husband's murder. Although she is not as sophisticated as Adler or as desperate as the Dark Lady, and although her position in the story is eclipsed when Holmes turns to her lover, Captain Croker, for the real story, she is an important addition to Doyle's collection of criminal women. She is absolutely willing to disregard the law (for which she has questionable respect because of its repressive stance vis-à-vis divorce) in order to protect Croker. She does not shirk from her resolve even when Holmes tells her he knows she is lying.

Though she has not murdered Sir Eustace herself, there seems little doubt that she would have done it given the right circumstances, since she had adequate motivation. David Brown speculates that some of her independence results from her national identity; South Australia, as she herself maintains, allowed women much greater autonomy than they enjoyed in England. In 1894, when English women won the right to vote in local elections, South Australian women were completely enfranchised.[4] But Doyle's point is more generic: women prevented by the law from escaping from intolerable husbands will find a way to circumvent the law.

Once again Holmes deliberately keeps his incriminating information from the police, as he had with the Dark Lady. He admires and protects Croker because of the captain's role as Lady Mary's deliverer, but his decision is a direct condemnation of the injustices women suffer from abusive men and rigid social codes. He comments: "Once or twice in my career I feel I have done more real harm by my discovery of the criminal than ever he had done by his crime. I have learned caution now, and I had rather play tricks with the law of England than with my own conscience."

Unlike the femmes fatales that the fin de siècle painters and writers produced, Doyle's criminal women are not lamias or mermaids but realistic adversaries worthy of Sherlock Holmes's intelligence. He is not smothered by them, or drowned, or even poisoned. True, he is impervious to their sexual charms, but he admires several and sympathizes with many of them. Unlike most of the male criminals, who forfeit respect, especially when they victimize women, Doyle's violent heroines are not threats to the social order but avengers of misuse. Certainly there is chauvinism implicit in such a distinction, but Doyle, more explicitly than any writer before, anticipates the persuasive criminal defenses in the twentieth century of women who have killed abusive men.

AFTERWORD

When women murdered in Victorian fiction, they killed to escape from intolerable subservience to a man's will, to avoid the threat of social disgrace and ostracism, or to insure their financial security. Many novelists were more comfortable thinking that if women could tolerate or subvert abuse, they did, obviating the need for violence. But from Dickens to Doyle, with incremental resonance, novelists sympathized with the killers even if they did not openly advocate their decisions and invariably punished them for their assertiveness.

It is not surprising that there are so few women killers. The fiction was more or less realistic; there simply were not large numbers of women killers in Victorian society, any more than there are in our own time. The possibility that dozens, or even hundreds, of unpleasant husbands, annoying children, or demanding elderly relatives died from poison in their soup or ground glass in their gruel is fantasy, despite the easy accessibility of the means and the understandable temptation of the ends. At the same time, everything the novelists described happened: unmarried mothers did kill their infants, abused wives their husbands, abandoned women their lovers.

It can be frustrating for us, though, that the novelists concentrated on individuals without looking beyond the individual to the larger causes for crime endemic in Victorian society and that they extrapolated from middle-class examples truths that did not apply to the working-class women who have always made up the bulk of the criminal population. Because the novelists described domestic tensions, they seemed to feel justified in ignoring the political implications of their women's deeds. But a woman does not have to kill the king or the governor of the Bastille, as Madame DeFarge did, to commit a political crime. The violent strikes these women characters make against abusive individuals and an inequitable system are not only private battles with Pyrrhic victories. By their very nature, they become public acts. The Victorian killers with socioeconomic motives strike the first blows in a very long war for gender equality. For the novelists recognized, as their contemporary social scientists did not, that women who killed might be anomalies but they were not abnormal, degenerate, or more irrational than men.

NOTES

Introduction

1. See Richard Barickman, Susan MacDonald, and Myra Stark, *Corrupt Relations: Dickens, Thackeray, Trollope, Collins, and the Victorian Sexual System* (New York: Columbia Univ. Press, 1982), 9, for a related discussion of "bad" women who operate within their ordinary "female" roles to challenge the idea that "good" women had any power in Victorian society.

2. See the introduction to Judith L. Newton, *Women, Power and Subversion* (1981; reprint, New York: Metheun, 1985); Sandra Gilbert and Susan Gubar, *The Madwoman in the Attic* (New Haven: Yale Univ. Press, 1979); and other recent works on women's protests in the Victorian era.

3. Mary S. Hartman, *Victorian Murderesses* (New York: Schocken Books, 1977), 2.

4. Rachel Brownstein, *Becoming a Heroine: Reading About Women in Novels* (New York: Viking Press, 1982), xxiii.

5. See Catherine R. Stimpson, "Introduction," in *Feminist Issues in Literary Scholarship*, ed. Shari Benstock (Bloomington: Indiana Univ. Press, 1987), 5; and Alice Jardine, "Gynesis," *Diacritics* 12 (Summer 1982): 54-65. See also Annette Kolodny, "Some Notes on Defining a 'Feminist Literature,' " *Critical Inquiry* 2 (Autumn 1975): 75-92, and a discussion of Kolodny's ideas in Jardine, "Gynesis," 56.

6. John Reed, *Victorian Conventions* (Athens: Ohio Univ. Press, 1975), 74.

7. Almost all feminist scholarship in the last twenty years, as well as a significant proportion of more traditional criticism, has discounted the artificial distinctions between the genres. For particularly persuasive feminist explanations, see Jane Tompkins, *Sensational Designs* (New York: Oxford Univ. Press, 1985), and Flavia Alaya, "Feminists on Victorians: The Pardoning Frame of Mind," *Dickens Studies Annual* 15 (1986): 337-80.

8. Newton, *Women, Power and Subversion*, 13.

ONE. The Worst of Women

1. Richard Barickman, Susan MacDonald, and Myra Stark argue in *Corrupt Relations* (p. 54) that for a woman to act aggressively she must "usurp a male position of power" which as an aberrant act is ultimately self-destructive (which is also John Reed's view in *Victorian Conventions*). Earlier they observe that "by presenting the 'bad' woman as a victim of a cruelly oppressive sexual system, [Victorian novelists] undermine the orthodox position" on criminal women (p. 9).

2. Curiously, however, women were sometimes very supportive of women defendants in actual criminal cases. An assessment of the cases which provoked extensive female support would provide valuable insight into Victorian attitudes toward mitigating factors in criminal trials. As far as I know, a study like this has not been done.

3. Gilbert and Gubar, *Madwoman in the Attic*, 191, 197-201.

4. The link between womanly submissiveness and childbirth suffering takes on even greater meaning when the history of women's health is considered. Milton's first two wives died following confinement; so did many Victorian women. Although this subject invites an extensive examination, it does fall outside the limits of the present study.

5. Daniel Defoe, *Roxana* (1724; reprint, London: Oxford Univ. Press, 1964), 311.

6. A more sober, repressive view of the consequences of crime tied to illicit sexual pleasure or appetite is best illustrated by Abbé Prevost's *Histoire du Chevalier des Grieux et de Manon Lescaut* (1731), better known to modern audiences in Puccini's *Manon Lescaut* and Jules Massenet's *Manon*. The passionate love affair of the young couple, Manon and the Chevalier, flourishes for a time; the two support each other, she as a courtesan and he as a card-sharp. After perpetrating a series of deceits and swindles, Manon is exiled to Louisiana, and the Chevalier accompanies her; but unlike Moll Flanders, Manon dies a lonely, miserable death as the consequence of her beauty, her crimes, and her sexuality.

7. See Keith Hollingsworth, *The Newgate Novel, 1830-1847* (Detroit: Wayne State Univ. Press, 1963). Benjamin Franklin Fisher IV, in "The Residual Gothic Impulse, 1824-1873" (in *Horror Literature: A Core Reference Guide*, ed. Marshall B. Tymm [New York: R.R. Bowker Company, 1981], 176-220), calls Newgate fiction "a naturalized branch of the Gothic in which the supernatural was routinely reduced to the brutalities of the prison" (p. 191).

8. See Judith Wilt, *Ghosts of the Gothic* (Princeton: Princeton Univ. Press, 1980), 12, 181ff.

9. Elaine Showalter, *A Literature of Their Own* (Princeton: Princeton Univ. Press, 1977), 120.

10. Elizabeth Hardwick, *Seduction and Betrayal* (New York: Random House, 1970), 182-87.

11. A more destructive, though seemingly innocent, variation of this feminine character type evokes a powerful literary tension between the conventional view

of a foolish woman and the more critical perspective of the novelist. Thus, the Princess Casamassima, in Henry James's novel, holds revolutionary but highly romanticized political views. As a result, she brings chaos into a society she does not understand; she is morally, if not legally, responsible for Hyacinth Robinson's suicide. Yet from her own perspective and that of her society, her fault lies only in her foolishness and egocentricity. Criminal guilt is not involved.

Two. Women and Victorian Law

1. Albie Sachs and Joan Hoff Wilson, *Sexism and the Law* (Oxford: Martin Robertson and Company, 1978), 53; and Newton, *Women, Power, and Subversion*, 4.

2. Havelock Ellis, *The Criminal* (1890; reprint, Montclair, N.J.: Patterson Smith, 1973), 261.

3. Richard Altick, *Victorian Studies in Scarlet* (New York: Norton and Company, 1970), passim. See also, Altick, *Deadly Encounters: Two Victorian Sensations* (Philadelphia: Univ. of Pennsylvania Press, 1986) and Thomas Boyle, *Black Swine in the Sewers of Hampstead: Beneath the Surface of Victorian Sensationalism* (New York: Viking Press, 1989).

4. Peter C. Hoffer and N.E. Hull, *Murdering Mothers: Infanticide in England and New England, 1558-1803* (New York: New York Univ. Press, 1981), 159; *London's Underworld*, ed. Peter Quennell (London: Spring Books, 1950), 52, reports Henry Mayhew's statistic that there were 1,130 inquests on murdered children between 1855 and 1860; C.A. Fyffe, "The Punishment of Infanticide," *Nineteenth Century* 1 (1877): 587, says 5,000 baby deaths were subject to coroner's inquests each year.

5. Abortion was not murder in common law, but after 1861, with the Offences against the Person Act, it became illegal to induce abortion either on one's self or on another person. Abortion to save the mother's life was legal after 1929 and was sometimes interpreted to include the mother's psychological well being. See Madeleine Simms and Keith Hindell, *Abortion Law Reformed* (London: Peter Owen, 1971), and J.W. Cecil Turner, ed., *Russell on Crime*, 12th ed. (London: Sweet and Maxwell, 1986), 1:601ff. The Abortion Act of 1967 allowed medical abortions in cases of risk to the mother and/or the family or if the fetus would produce a handicapped baby. See Ian McLean and Peter Morrish, *Harris's Criminal Law*, 22d ed. (London: Sweet and Maxwell, 1973), 448f.

6. C.A. Fyffe, "The Punishment of Infanticide," 584.

7. Sir James Fitzjames Stephen, "Variations in the Punishment of Crime," *Nineteenth Century* 17 (1885): 760.

8. Elizabeth Wolstenholme-Elmy, *Infant Mortality: Its Causes and Remedies* (Manchester: A. Ireland, 1871), 38.

9. Sachs and Wilson, *Sexism and the Law*, 44.

10. William Douglas Morrison, *Crime and Its Causes* (London: Swan Sonnenschein, 1891), 151.

11. William A. Guy, "On the Executions for Murder That Have Taken Place

in England and Wales During the Last Seventy Years," *Journal of the Statistical Society* 38 (1875): 480.

12. Patrick Wilson, *Murderess* (London: Michael Joseph, 1971), 315.

13. Morrison, *Crime and Its Causes*, 179.

14. Wilson, *Murderess*, 315.

15. Millicent Fawcett, *Mr. Fitzjames Stephen on the Position of Women* (London: Macmillan, 1873), 14. See also "Privilege versus Justice to Women," *Westminster Review* 152 (1899): 128-41.

16. "Little Women," *Saturday Review*, 25 April 1868, 545-46. Eliza Lynn Linton, "Partisans of Wild Women," *Nineteenth Century* 31 (March 1892): 457. See also, Linton, "Are Good Women Characterless?" *Forum* 6 (February 1889): 644-52.

17. Quoted in Hartman, *Victorian Murderesses*, 126.

18. Morrison, *Crime and Its Causes*, 152.

19. Keith Thomas, "The Double Standard," *Journal of the History of Ideas* 20 (1959): 202.

20. *Times*, 28 August 1872, p. 9, cols. 4-5.

21. Sir James Fitzjames Stephen, *A Digest of the Criminal Law*, 7th ed., ed. Sir Herbert Stephen and Sir Harry Lushington Stephen (London: Sweet and Maxwell, 1926), 201-24; R.N. Gooderson, "Defences in Double Harness," in *Reshaping the Criminal Law*, ed. P.R. Glazerbrook (London: Stevens & Sons, 1978), 143.

22. J.W. Kaye, "Outrages on Women," *North British Review* 25 (May 1856): 247-52. See also Frances Power Cobbe, *The Life of Frances Power Cobbe by Herself* (London: Richard Bently, 1894), 2:73.

23. Herbert Spencer, *The Study of Sociology*, introduction by Talcott Parsons (Ann Arbor: Univ. of Michigan Press, 1961), 344. Spencer also maintains that women can learn to please violent men and so diffuse their brutality.

24. Elizabeth Wolstenholme-Elmy, *The Criminal Code in Its Relation to Women* (Manchester: Alex. Ireland, Printers, 1880), 5.

25. Mary Carpenter, *Our Convicts* (1864; reprint, Montclair, N.J.: Patterson Smith, 1969), 207.

26. "Little Women," 545.

27. Alan Harding, *A Social History of English Law* (Baltimore: Penguin Books, 1966), 360.

28. Hartman, *Victorian Murderesses*, 133.

29. Wolstenholme-Elmy, *Criminal Code in Its Relation to Women*, 16.

30. Allison Morris, *Women, Crime and Criminal Justice* (London: Basil Blackwell, 1987), 135.

31. Hermann Mannheim, *Comparative Criminology* (Boston: Houghton Mifflin, 1965), 691.

32. See Harding, *Social History of English Law*, 362.

33. Hargreave L. Adam, *Women and Crime* (London: Werner Lourie, 1914), 17.

34. Susan Jacoby, *Wild Justice: The Evolution of Revenge* (New York: Harper and Row, 1983), 187.

35. Carol Smart, *Women, Crime, and Criminology* (London: Routledge and Kegan Paul, 1976), 34.

36. Guy, "On the Executions," 466.

37. *The Echo*, 11 January 1869, p. 1.

38. H.B. Irving, ed., *The Trial of Mrs. Maybrick* (Edinburgh and London: William Hodge, 1912), 327-33.

39. Irving, *Trial*, 349.

40. Irving, *Trial*, 351.

41. Sir Leslie Stephen, *The Life of Sir James Fitzjames Stephen*, 2d ed. (London: Smith, Elder, 1895), xxx.

42. Francoise Basch, *Relative Creatures: Victorian Women in Society and the Novel*, trans. Anthony Rudolf (New York: Schocken Books, 1974), 24.

43. Morrison, *Crime and Its Causes*, 206.

44. James Boswell, *Journal of a Tour to the Hebrides with Samuel Johnson, LL.D.*, ed. Ralph H. Isham. Quoted in *Enlightened England*, rev. ed., ed. Wylie Sypher (New York: Norton, 1962), 915.

45. J.J. Tobias, *Crime and Industrial Society in the 19th Century* (London: Batsford, 1967), 7. For a contrasting interpretation of Victorian crime statistics and the relationship of crime to economic conditions, see V.A.C. Gatrell and T.B. Hadden, "Criminal Statistics and Their Interpretation," in *Nineteenth-century Society: Essays in the Use of Quantitative Methods for the Study of Social Data*, ed. E.A. Wrigley (Cambridge: Cambridge Univ. Press, 1972), 336-96.

46. Wolstenholme-Elmy, *Infant Mortality*, 14-19.

47. Susan S.M. Edwards, *Female Sexuality and the Law* (Oxford: Martin Robertson, 1981), 39.

48. Carpenter, *Our Convicts*, 207. For a similar view more passionately expressed, see Mrs. M.E. Owens, "Criminal Women," *Cornhill Magazine* 14 (August 1866): 152-60.

49. Luke Owen Pike, *A History of Crime In England* (London: Smith, Elder, 1876), 2:527.

50. Carpenter, *Our Convicts*, 209.

51. Quoted in Marvin E. Wolfgang, *Patterns in Criminal Homicide* (New York: John Wiley, 1966), 209.

52. L.A.J. Quetelet, *A Treatise on Man and the Development of His Faculties* (1842; reprint, Gainesville, Fla.: Scholars' Facsimiles and Reprints, 1969), 82-96.

53. Edwards, *Female Sexuality*, 52.

THREE. Charles Dickens

1. See Philip Collins, *Dickens and Crime* (Bloomington: Indiana Univ. Press, 1968), for a comprehensive discussion of Dickens's attitudes toward crime in society.

2. Critical debate about the credibility and validity of Dickens's women characters is voluminous. See, for instance, Michael Slater, *Dickens and Women*

(Palo Alto, Calif.: Stanford Univ. Press, 1983); Gilbert and Gubar on the repressed rage characteristic of idealized women, *Madwoman in the Attic*, 26; and articles in *Dickens Studies Annual, Victorian Studies*, and other professional journals.

3. See Charles Dickens, *Sketches By Boz*, chap. 5, 6, 16, 22, 25 ("Scenes"); chap. 11 ("Characters"); and chap. 12 ("Tales") for work discussing the influence of poverty and deprivation on women's lives.

4. See chapter 2 of this book for a discussion of men's legal right to beat their wives and children. Estella Havisham faces the same dilemma in *Great Expectations*; she too is worn out by the trauma of an abusive spouse; but she is luckier than Nancy because Bantley Drummle is killed by a horse he has abused.

5. See Dickens's preface to the 1841 edition of *Oliver Twist*.

6. Dickens, still working out his own views, describes crime as the consequence of different things in the novel. Although Nancy is driven to it by her environment and Oliver by duress, Sikes and Fagin seem innately and inherently evil. In subsequent novels, Dickens increasingly stressed the impact of social circumstances on different characters to explain their behavior.

7. Paul C. Squires, "Charles Dickens as Criminologist," *Journal of the American Institute of Criminal Law and Criminology* 29 (1938-39): 187-88. Squires argues that her behavior is exceptional, not typical.

8. Slater, *Dickens and Women*, 221.

9. Beth Kalikoff, *Murder and Moral Decay in Victorian Popular Literature* (Ann Arbor: UMI Research Press, 1986), 44ff. See also Hollingsworth, *Newgate Novel*, 148ff.

10. Nina Auerbach, "Dickens and Dombey: A Daughter After All," *Dickens Studies Annual* 5 (1976): 109, stresses the phallic power of the train which kills Carker. While I find the overall association of the railroad and masculine energy persuasive, I think the image here is empowered by its association with Edith Dombey, who is full of destructive energy. See Jenni Calder, *Women and Marriage in Victorian Fiction* (New York: Oxford Univ. Press, 1976), 112

11. Louise Yellin, "Strategies for Survival: Florence and Edith in *Dombey and Son*," *Victorian Studies* 22 (Spring 1979): 319. Yellin's overall reading of the text, however, is compelling, especially her discussion of Edith's latent violence illustrated when she smashes the hand Carker has kissed against the mantle until it bleeds. Other readers respond differently to the Dombeys. See Judith Newton, "Making—and Remaking—History: Another Look at Patriarchy," in *Feminist Issues in Literary Scholarship*, ed. Sheri Benstock (Bloomington: Indiana Univ. Press, 1987), 131-34; and Slater, *Dickens and Women*, 260ff. as examples.

12. It is generally agreed that Swiss-born Manning was Dickens's primary source for the details of Hortense's character, including her foreign birth and her fiery temper. Note that the overt sexual component (i.e., lover as victim) was omitted in Dickens's treatment.

13. After the Manning execution, which he watched, Dickens became a vehement opponent of capital punishment. See Collins, *Dickens and Crime*, 240.

It is reasonable to assume that Hortense's inevitable punishment is glossed over to avoid describing such a scene.

14. Jaggers's placing Estella with Miss Havisham and his refusal to let Molly know what has become of her child strike the modern reader as intolerable arrogance. The entire subject of the lack of maternal instincts in criminal women as evidence of their abnormality is more explicit in other novelists. See, for instance, the discussion of George Eliot's Hetty Sorrell below.

15. See *Bleak House*, chap. 23, for evidence that Dickens had been thinking about the French Revolution as the appropriate milieu for violent women.

16. Readers aware of Dickens's attitude toward the inhumanity of public executions and their effect on the audience realize the import of DeFarge's delight in watching the beheadings.

17. Miss Pross, English to her fingertips, curses DeFarge with this epithet, *A Tale of Two Cities*, book 3, chap. 14.

FOUR. George Eliot

1. Carol Christ, in "Aggression and Providential Death in George Eliot's Fiction," *Novel* 9 (Winter 1976): 130-40, links Wybrow's death and the convenient deaths of other characters in Eliot's works. Killing people off, she says, is Eliot's method of resolving intolerable situations. Christ's emphasis, while it does not consider the criminal potential in the characters left behind, does focus important attention on the relationship between wishing to do violence (or murder) and suffering guilt when the deed is done by providence.

2. See Christine E. Rasche, "Etiological Perspectives on Women and Homicide," *Women and Criminal Justice* 2 (1990). Victim-precipitated homicide means that the victim (in domestic violence cases, usually a man) has so provoked the killer that the violent response is justifiable, or a defense equivalent to self-defense. The concept was first articulated by Hans Von Hentig, "Remarks on the Interaction of Perpetrator and Victim," *Journal of Criminal Law and Criminology* 31 (1940): 303-9.

3. Women sometimes did flee abusive marriages in novels of the period, as they had in eighteenth-century fiction, but rarely to improved circumstances unless they had the financial and emotional support of family or friends. A revealing contrast is provided by Anne Brontë's *The Tenant of Wildfell Hall* and her sister Emily Brontë's *Wuthering Heights*. In the former, Helen Graham, with her brother's aid and comfort, is able to make a new life for herself while Isabella Heathcliff struggles and dies in penury and bitterness. Alcoholic women are only rarely the central characters in Victorian fiction; one example is Julie Kavanaugh's *Beatrice* (1865).

4. Nina Auerbach, *The Woman and the Demon* (Cambridge, Mass.: Harvard Univ. Press, 1982), 63-108; Bram Dijkstra, *Idols of Perversity* (New York: Oxford Univ. Press, 1986), *passim*.

5. Eliot, *Letters*, 2:344-45, quoted in Gordon S. Haight, *George Eliot: A Biography* (New York: Oxford Univ. Press, 1968), 234.

6. Eliot, *Letters*, 2:353, quoted in Haight, *George Eliot*, 238.

7. Haight, *George Eliot*, 249. Eliot discussed her sources in *Letters*, 2:502, although she was adamant that her characters were not modeled on real people. She had heard her aunt's story in 1839 and began the novel in October 1857, having decided against making it the fourth story in *Scenes of Clerical Life*. See also *A George Eliot Miscellany*, ed. F.B. Pinion (London: Macmillan, 1982), 107.

8. 9 August 1856. The pattern of acquittal which he denounced with such fervor was not new: since about 1740, indictments and convictions for infanticide had fallen dramatically in England, and in 1803 a repressively severe law, which had been in force since 1624, was repealed as a pragmatic response to the fact that juries were not convicting infanticide defendants even when such cases reached the courts.

9. Among the key provisions of the old law were the presumption of guilt when an illegitimate child died or disappeared and the mother had not made preparations for its birth (like providing clothing) or confided in anyone.

10. Elizabeth Gaskell, *The Manufacturing Population of England* (London, 1833), quoted in Keith Thomas, "The Double Standard," *Journal of the History of Ideas* 20 (1959): 206. Illicit pregnancies in middle- and upper-class families were invariably covered up, and urges to murder, which Eliot alludes to in the character of Mrs. Transome in *Felix Holt, Radical*, are restrained.

11. In the 1861 Offenses against the Person Act strict new guidelines were provided for punishing concealment of birth, but in *R. v. May* (1867; 10 Cox 448) the court found a woman could not be convicted for concealing the birth of a baby she abandoned alive in the corner of a field although the child subsequently died. See J.W. Cecil Turner, *Russell on Crime*, vol. 1 (London: Sweet and Maxwell, 1986), 606.

12. See Dorothy Van Ghent, "Adam Bede," in *The English Novel: Form and Function* (New York: Harper and Row, 1961), 178, for the view that Hetty's crime and punishment were a "frivolity" that brought "irreparable damage" to the community. See also U.C. Knoepflmacher, *George Eliot's Early Novels: The Limits of Realism* (Berkeley: Univ. of California Press, 1968), 118-20, 123.

13. According to Henry James, the novel would have been stronger if Hetty had been executed. See James, "The Novels of George Eliot," *A Century of George Eliot Criticism*, ed. Gordon S. Haight (Boston: Houghton Mifflin, 1965), 47.

14. Joan Mannheimer, "Murderous Mothers: The Problem of Parenting in the Victorian Novel," *Feminine Studies* 5 (Fall 1979): 541, 543.

15. Calder, *Women and Marriage in Victorian Fiction*, 157.

16. Judith Wilt, *Ghosts of the Gothic*, 209.

17. See Auerbach, *Woman and the Demon*, and Elisabeth G. Gitter, "The Power of Women's Hair in the Victorian Imagination," *PMLA* 99 (October 1984): 943.

18. Some critics suggest lesbian overtones; my reading is that girls ignorant of sexual matters are often repulsed, and that Eliot was much more likely to be commenting on the appalling consequences of prudery than on lesbianism.

19. Eliot made the same point in *Romola* (1864), that the unhappy wife and the abandoned mistress are two sides of the same coin.

20. Christ, "Agression and Providential Death," 140.

FIVE. Mary Elizabeth Braddon

1. Margaret Oliphant, "Novels," *Blackwood's Edinburgh Magazine* 102 (September 1967): 257-80. See also Leslie Stephen, "The Decay of Murder," *Cornhill Magazine* 20 (December 1869): 722-33, and A. Innes Shand, "Crime in Fiction," *Blackwood's Edinburgh Magazine* 148 (August 1890): 172-89.

2. See Thomas Boyle, *Black Swine in the Sewers of Hampstead* (New York: Viking Books, 1989) for a discussion of the influence of mid-century crime reporting on the plots and language of the emerging sensation novel.

3. Showalter, *Literature of Their Own*, 165ff.

4. Despite the fact that later in the novel Braddon refers to William Holman Hunt, an artist who often used doubling images on his paintings, to reassert the portrait's depiction of Lucy's dual personality, there is no Hunt work as evocative of the sense of feminine evil that Braddon is trying to create as either Rosetti's painting of Lucrezia Borgia (1860-61) or Burne-Jones's of Sidonia von Bork (1860).

5. Gitter, "Power of Women's Hair," 943.

6. For a Victorian reaction to Lady Audley, see Shand, "Crime in Fiction," 188. Audley is labelled a "moral monstrosity," but Braddon is praised for her readability and credibility. "We are inclined to accept all she writes as gospel. If it is not true it ought to be, so great is the air of *vraisemblance*."

7. The novel reflects the ability of families with the financial or social resources to block or manipulate police investigations and "spare" their women the public disgrace of judicial proceedings. Constance Kent's case provides an interesting illustration. Whatever his motive, Kent's father kept the local police from investigating the scene of the crime for several hours, joined them in their examination of the physical evidence, and was made privy to their findings and suspicions (see Hartman, *Victorian Murderesses*, 118 and *passim*, for discussion of the details of the case). When Constance was not indicted—although she was the prime suspect—he promptly sent her to a convent school in France where she was kept, under a false name, for three years. His machinations put Robert Audley's behavior in Braddon's novel in perspective.

8. Showalter, *Literature of Their Own*, 166, argues persuasively that Audley was not insane and that her guilty "secret" was that she was a highly competent and assertive woman clever enough to hide her brains behind her physical charms.

9. *The Black Swan*, in Brown, *The Dwale Bluth*, vol. 2 (London: Tinsley Brothers, 1876). To get the novel published the first time (as *Gabriel Denver* in 1873), Brown mitigated Denver's guilt by changing the vengeful wife to an unloved fiancée and added a happy ending, but retained his candid description of the powerful physical attraction between Denver and Laura Conway and the destructive fury of the abandoned woman.

10. James Aschcroft Noble, *Morality in English Fiction* (Liverpool: W and J Arnold, 1887), 53.

11. See Winifred Hughes, *The Maniac in the Cellar: Sensation Novels of the 1860's* (Princeton: Princeton Univ. Press, 1980), and Sally Mitchell, *The Fallen Angel*, for perceptive reassessments. In this context it is interesting to read George Eliot's "Silly Novels by Lady Novelists," *Westminster Review* 66 (1856): 442-61.

12. The puzzle that women criminals posed for nineteenth-century novelists and their audiences is encapsulated by E.S. Dallas's *The Gay Science* (1866), an exposition and critique of the science of criticism. Before he tackles the way women are described in contemporary novels, Dallas defends sensation fiction as legitimate literature, observing that it differs from respectable literature "solely in the relation of the characters pourtrayed [sic] to the actions described," and insisting that neither the serious novel's emphasis on the control a character exerts on his circumstances nor the sensation novel's suggestion that character is controlled by event is wholly true or wholly false. He attacks the grounds on which sensation fiction is damned: "To show man as the sport of circumstance may be a depressing view of human nature; but it is not fair to regard it as immoral nor to denounce it as utterly untrue" (xvii).

When he turns to a discussion of the feminine influence which "pervades" literature, he forgets his own observations about veracity and the mirroring of society. Novelists "deny truth" if they make women central to the action because that is not the way things are, he says. He sees no irony in his own observation that the first appearance of a woman in literature—Eve in the Garden of Eden—is also the first instance of unfeminine behavior. His eventual point, however, is a reluctant acknowledgment that by concentrating on women, especially women of action, the novelists became increasingly interested in the private individual rather than a larger-than-life character, not only as hero(ine) but also as villain(ess).

Six. Wilkie Collins

1. See Hartman, *Victorian Murderesses*, 179, 213.

2. Hughes, *Maniac in the Cellar*, 46.

3. Collins, in his prefatory note to *Armadale*, included in the 1866 and subsequent editions, is particularly harsh in condeming the rigidity of Victorian morality.

4. U.C. Knoepflmacher, "The Counterworld of Victorian Fiction," in *The Worlds of Victorian Fiction*, ed. Jerome H. Buckley (Cambridge, Mass.: Harvard Univ. Press, 1975), 368, discusses the dark themes of Collins's fiction in a different context.

5. Boyle, *Black Swine*, 103-15.

6. Barbara T. Gates, "Wilkie Collins Suicides: 'Truth As It Is In Nature,' " *Dickens Studies Annual* 12 (1983): 305.

7. Cuff's views are not only sexist but classist. See Nicole Hahn Rafter and Elizabeth Anne Stanko, *Judge, Lawyer, Victim, Thief* (Boston: Northeastern

164   NOTES TO PAGES 118-132

Univ. Press, 1982), 51, for a discussion of the biases of the Victorian reform movement. One potentially explosive subject Collins declines to elaborate is the explicitly revolutionary threats Rosanna's friend Lucy Yolland makes against men, the upper classes, and the rich—radical feminine politics, Victorian style.

8. There is one superb, but unintentional, irony, however, in Collins's assault on abusive men. The least likable woman in the novel, Lady Lundie, is not only a busybody but a shrew; she makes a fatal error in scorning Anne, thereby earning her brother-in-law's (and the narrator's) hatred. But when the estimable Sir Patrick Lundie tries to imagine how Lady Lundie might be made manageable, he remarks: "If she had been the wife of a bricklayer, she is the sort of woman who would have been kept in perfect order by a vigorous and regular application of her husband's fist" (chap. 26).

9. Cobbe, *Life of Frances Power Cobbe*, 2:70-71. Cobbe had covered the story for the newspaper *The Echo* from Friday, 15 January 1869, through Tuesday, 19 January 1869. Between 3 February and 8 April of the same year, the *Times* reported three other cases of women assaulting or killing (presumably abusive) men.

SEVEN. Thomas Hardy

1. Michael Millgate, *Thomas Hardy: A Biography* (New York: Random House, 1982), 192. One source for *Tess* was the experience of the Hardys' young housemaid, Jane Phillips, who disappeared in the summer of 1877, and whose illegitimate baby died shortly after its birth later that same year. Millgate suggests that Hardy had also heard the story that Phillips had baptized her baby privately before its death and asserts that Phillips's story personified "the sheer power of sexuality and the gross injustices of a social system which thrust upon the woman the burden of sexual responsibility and guilt."

2. Thomas Hardy, *Letters*, collected by Richard Little Purdy and Michael Millgate (Oxford and New York: Clarendon Press, 1978), 251.

3. Ruth Milberg-Kay, *Thomas Hardy—Myths of Sexuality* (New York: John Jay Press, 1983), 58.

4. Readings of the text which blame Tess for her tragedy are inherently antifeminist; a parallel view suggests that abused wives invite punishment by not living up to their husband's (legitimate) expectations.

5. See Henry Mayhew, "Prostitution in London," in *London Underworld*, ed. Peter Quennell (London: Spring Books, 1950), 31-128.

6. Hardy, *Letters*, 221.

7. The same charges were made in the sensational accusations of murder against Florence Bravo in 1876, Adelaide Bartlett in 1886, and Mary Wheeler Pearcey in 1890; murder was the result of the extramarital sexual experience of the accused.

8. See Hartman, *Victorian Murderesses*, 215ff. She cites evidence that Maybrick was the victim of repeated physical abuse.

9. H.B. Irving, ed., *The Trial of Florence Maybrick* (Edinburgh and London: William Hodge, 1912), 350.

10. Irving, *Trial*, 352.

11. The "leniency" of Maybrick's commuted sentence outraged Queen Victoria, who was convinced of Maybrick's guilt. Finally, in 1904, the prisoner was freed by order of King Edward VII.

12. Two other causes célèbres of 1889 emphasized the fragility of marriage and its potential for misery—the London production of Ibsen's *A Doll's House* and the divorce petition filed by Captain O'Shea against his wife Kitty because of her relationship with the Irish leader Parnell. See William Rutland, *Thomas Hardy: A Study of His Writings and Their Background* (New York: Russell and Russell, 1962), 250f.

13. The more powerful motive, first included in the 1892 edition but later obscured, is her pathetic statement "He bought me," later simply "He———." He had; of that there is no question.

14. Adultery was one of the commandments Hardy called an "unbreakable" in "Candor in English Fiction," *New Review* 2 (January 1890): 6-21.

15. Thomas Hardy, *Tess of the d'Urbervilles*, ed. Juliet Grindle and Simon Gatrell (New York: Oxford Univ. Press, 1983), 26f, 32.

16. Michael Millgate, *Thomas Hardy: His Career as a Novelist* (New York: Random House, 1971), 280.

17. Millgate, *Career*, 265. The Maybrick trial (1889) and its aftermath, as I have said, were a travesty of justice and humanity.

18. Auerbach, *Woman and the Demon*, 170.

19. If the murder scene is passed over briefly, Tess's trial and execution are completely ignored. Perhaps, like Dickens, Hardy had been so appalled by the execution of a woman, in this case that of Martha Brown, which he witnessed in August 1856 (Millgate, *Career*, 267 and note), that he was unwilling to describe such a death in fiction.

EIGHT. Arthur Conan Doyle

1. Doyle's women criminals are consistently described as "exotic" or "foreign." For example, the woman killer in the "Adventure of the Golden Pincenez" is Russian, and the one in "Adventure of the Second Stain" is French-Creole. Elise, the accomplice to murder in "Adventure of the Engineer's Thumb," is German, and Isadora Klein, a Spaniard married to a German in "Adventure of the Three Gables," eagerly arranges for violent assaults on anybody who interferes with her plans. There are, as well, guilty Greeks, South Americans, and several citizens of the United United States, including the incomparable Adler. It is relevant that Adelaide Bartlett and Florence Maybrick, the defendants in two of the most sensational criminal cases of the 1880s, were not native Englishwomen.

2. Catherine Belsey, "Constructing the Subject: Deconstructing the Text,"

in *Feminist Criticism and Social Change*, ed. Judith Newton and Deborah Rosenfelt (New York: Metheun, 1985), 62.

3. Ian Ousby, *The Bloodhounds of Heaven* (Cambridge, Mass.: Harvard Univ. Press, 1976), 167, comments that sexual danger introduces a note of hysteria into Doyle's writing.

4. David Brown, "Mary Fraser of Adelaide," *Baker Street Journal* 35 (September 1985): 147-52.

BIBLIOGRAPHICAL NOTE

The primary literary texts cited in this study are, with few exceptions, readily accessible. The works by Dickens, Eliot, Collins, Hardy, and Doyle appear in various paperback editions; so do Braddon's *Lady Audley's Secret*, Defoe's *Moll Flanders*, and the literary classics discussed in chapter 1. College, university, and research libraries have editions of Defoe's *Roxana*, of Gissing, LeFanu, and Charles Reade, and of the other novelists who are considered briefly. Because standard scholarly editions exist for some but not all of the novels, because individual readers will have various editions of the novels, and because I am interested primarily in a contextual analysis of the characters and themes rather than a close reading of texts, I have provided references to chapters rather than to pages in specific editions. It seemed the most consistent and appropriate approach.

Some sensation novels discussed in chapter 5 have not been reprinted since they went out of general circulation and so may be difficult to locate except in large repository libraries; these including Mary Elizabeth Braddon's *Joshua Haggard's Daughter* (London: John Maxwell, 1876; New York: Harper, 1877) and *Taken at the Flood* (London: John Maxwell, 1874; New York, Harper, 1874); Oliver Madox Brown's *The Black Swan*, printed with Brown's *The Dwale Bluth*, volume 2 (London: Tinsley Brothers, 1876); and Helen Mathers's *The Eye of Fate* (London: Ward, Lock and Co., n.d.) and *Murder or Manslaughter* (London: George Routledge and Sons, 1885).

In addition to the novels I have included in the present study, there are dozens of others with female criminals—some guilty as charged, some falsely accused, and some who get away with murder. Among the more interesting are F. Anstey [Thomas Anstey Gutherie], *The Statement of Stella Maberley* (London: T. Fisher Unwin, 1896); Frank

Barrett, *The Woman of the Iron Bracelets* (London: Chatto & Windus, 1893); Lucy Clifford, *Mrs. Keith's Crime* (London: Richard Bentley and Son, 1885); Helen Mathers, *The Land of Leal* (London, 1878); and Alice Maud Meadows, *A Ticket of Leave Girl* (London: Digby, Long & Co., 1911). Robert Lee Wolff's *Nineteenth Century Fiction: A Bibliographical Catalogue on the Collection Formed by Robert Lee Wolff*, 4 vols. (New York: Garland, 1981-1985), provides an extensive list of nineteenth-century novels with provocative titles and discreetly lurid covers for anyone interested in uncovering more women killers. To my knowledge, however, there is no inclusive annotated bibliography of nineteenth-century fiction about women criminals. Myron Brightfield's *Victorian England in Its Novels (1840-1870)*, 4 vols., with an introduction by Gordon N. Ray (Los Angeles: Univ. of California Press, 1968), does a momumental job of surveying what he calls the "mass of historical and social information" that the fiction of those thirty years provides, but he pays relatively little attention to women and virtually none to criminal women.

I know of no other scholarly work that focuses directly on creative literature about women who kill. In a new book, *Domestic Crime in the Victorian Novel* (New York: St. Martin's Press, 1989), Anthea Trodd discusses some of the same fiction. I regret that its recent publication prevented my discussing her ideas in the text; sometimes we agree and sometimes our readings are quite disparate. Many writers have analyzed the Victorian fiction that is my primary subject. Within the framework of their larger interests they discuss crimes, criminals, and punishments, but generally treat each violent incident as a tragic anomaly or an example of a novelist's particular world view. Although I often disagree with their conclusions about the roles of women criminals, I consider indispensable Nina Auerbach, *Woman and the Demon* (Cambridge: Harvard Univ. Press, 1982), on Thomas Hardy's *Tess of the d'Urbervilles*; Richard Barickman, Susan MacDonald, and Myra Stark, *Corrupt Relations* (New York: Columbia Univ. Press, 1982), on Charles Dickens and Wilkie Collins; Catherine Belsey, "Constructing the Subject: Deconstructing the Text," in Judith Newton and Deborah Rosenfelt, eds., *Feminist Criticism and Social Change* (New York and London: Metheun, 1985), on Dickens's *Dombey and Son*; Carol Christ, "Aggression and Providential Death in Geroge Eliot's Fiction," *Novel* 9 (Winter 1976): 130-40, on Eliot; Sandra Gilbert and Susan Gubar, *The Madwoman in the Attic: The Woman Writer and the Nineteenth Century Imagination* (New Haven: Yale Univ. Press, 1979), on Eliot's *Adam Bede*; Elaine Showalter, *A Literature of Their Own*

(Princeton: Princeton Univ. Press, 1977), on M.E. Braddon's *Lady Audley's Secret*; Michael Slater, *Dickens and Women* (Stanford: Stanford Univ. Press, 1983), on *Dombey and Son* and *Bleak House*; and Louise Yellin, "Strategies for Survival: Florence and Edith in *Dombey and Son*," *Victorian Studies* 22 (Spring 1979): 297-319.

I found similarly indispensible several studies of Victorian literature and culture published in the 1970s, many of them feminist and all concerned with women's roles in society, which provided the background I needed for my discussion of women criminals. They include Françoise Basch's *Relative Creatures: Victorian Women in Society and the Novel*, trans. Anthony Rudolf (New York: Schocken Books, 1974); Jenni Calder's *Women and Marriage in Victorian Fiction* (New York: Oxford Univ. Press, 1976); Jean E. Kennard's *Victims of Convention* (Hamden, Conn.: Archon Books, 1978); P.J. Keating's *The Working Class in Victorian Fiction* (New York: Barnes & Noble, 1971); John Reed's *Victorian Conventions* (Athens: Ohio Univ. Press, 1975); Marlene Springer's collection *What Manner of Women: Essays on English and American Life and Literature* (New York: New York Univ. Press, 1977), which includes her essay "Angels and Other Women in Victorian Literature"; Patricia Stubbs's *Women and Fiction: Feminism and the Novel* (Sussex: Harvester Press, 1979); and Martha Vicinus's two unsurpassed collections of essays, *Suffer and Be Still* and *A Widening Sphere* (Bloomington: Indiana Univ. Press, 1972 and 1977). A more recent book, Judith Lowder Newton's *Women, Power and Subversion: Social Strategies in British Fiction, 1778-1860* (1981; reprint, New York: Metheun, 1985) is a cogent example of the important new readings of Victorian fiction that feminist criticism has produced.

Feminist criminology, like the critical analysis of the role of women in fiction, in the same time frame and with the similar intention of refuting the biases created by male-centered scholarship, is another major body of scholarship from which my own work has developed. My emphasis has been on British women criminals in the nineteenth century, but I have been fascinated by the universality of women's experiences with criminal justice systems described by American and British researchers. Dorie Klein's essay "The Etiology of Female Crime: A Review of the Literature," *Issues in Criminology* 8 (1973): 3-30, is a landmark in the field, as is Carol Smart's groundbreaking *Women, Crime, and Criminology* (London: Routledge & Kegan Paul, 1976). Although their conclusions have been radically reassessed, Freda Adler's *Sisters in Crime* (New York: McGraw-Hill, 1975), Rita Simon's *Women and Crime* (Lexington, Mass.: D.C. Heath, 1975), and their jointly edited *The Criminology of Deviant Women* (Boston: Houghton Mifflin, 1979) were in the vanguard of the new interest in women criminals that exploded in the 1970s. Among the British studies I have found particularly useful or thought-provoking are two volumes of the Law and Society Series edited by C.M. Campbell and Paul Wiles: Albie Sachs and Joan Hoff Wilson, *Sexism and the Law* (Oxford: Martin Robertson, 1978), and Susan S.M. Edwards, *Female Sexuality and the Law* (Oxford: Martin Robertson, 1981). Eileen B. Leonard, in *Women, Crime and Society* (New York: Longman, 1982); Frances Heidensohn, in *Women and Crime* (Basingstoke: Macmillan, 1985); and Allison Morris, in *Women, Crime and Criminal Justice* (Oxford and New York: Basil Blackwell, 1987) survey the field and provide comprehensive bibliographies.

Nicole Hahn Rafter's *Partial Justice: Women in State Prisons, 1800-1935* (Boston: Northeastern Univ. Press, 1985) analyzes the American woman's experience with the criminal justice system during the Victorian period, providing a particularly useful cross-cultural insight. *Judge, Lawyer, Victim, Thief*, a collection of essays Rafter edited with Elizabeth Stanko (Boston: Northeast Univ. Press, 1982) encompasses a myriad of disciplines and approaches to the study of women and crime. That interdisciplinary focus is a distinguishing mark of feminist criminology and an important influence on the conceptualization of my book.

Historical studies of women as criminals and victims have provided another perspective. Mary S. Hartman, in *Victorian Murderesses* (New York: Schocken Books, 1977), describes six middle-class British women (and six French women) implicated in murder during the Victorian period and discusses the social and legal environments in which their cases were assessed. Hartman's book and Ann Jones's polemical but fascinating analysis of American crime history in *Women Who Kill* (New York: Holt, Rinehart and Winston, 1980) provide ample evidence of the motives of and consequences for murderous women. Patrick Wilson's *Murderess* (London: Michael Joseph, 1971) is less scholarly but full of interesting bits of information; and Susan Jacoby, writing about men as well as women in *Wild Justice: The Evolution of Revenge* (New York: Harper and Row, 1983), provokes the reader into thinking about crime in its cultural context.

Richard D. Altick's classic *Victorian Studies in Scarlet* (New York: Norton, 1970) describes the Victorian obsession with crime, especially violent crimes or crimes with sexual indiscretions; and in a very recent book, *Black Swine in the Sewers of Hampstead* (New York: Viking

Books, 1989), Thomas Boyle examines Victorian newspapers' sensationalized descriptions of crimes and trials as a source for the sensation fiction of the era. Popular fiction featuring criminal violence is assessed in its cultural context in Beth Kalikoff's *Murder and Moral Decay in Victorian Popular Literature* (Ann Arbor: UMI Research Press, 1986). Using Boyle and Kalikoff in conjunction with Winifred Hughes's more traditional literary analysis of the same nontraditional corpus of fiction, *The Maniac in the Cellar* (Princeton: Princeton Univ. Press, 1980), emphasizes the long-ignored complexity of Victorian popular fiction. Elaine Showalter's *The Female Malady: Women, Madness, and English Culture, 1830-1980* (New York: Pantheon Books, 1985) provides an insightful analysis of the alacrity with which Victorian women were labeled "mad" when their behavior defied the ideal.

I also found a rich store of primary material on Victorian women and crime, some of it contained in contemporary histories of crime and justice such as Luke Owen Pike's *A History of Crime in England* (London: Smith, Elder and Company, 1876) and William Douglas Morrison's *Crime and Its Causes* (London: Swan Sonnenschein, 1891), and some written as journal essays. Women whose moral indignation was aroused by their own unjust treatment or by the treatment of other women wrote powerful indictments of the gender-biased and class-biased Victorian judicial system. Caroline Norton, herself an abused wife denied the right to see her children after a bitter divorce, wrote *English Laws for Women in the Nineteenth Century* (1854; reprint, Westport, Conn.: Hyperion Press, 1981), one of the earliest summaries of the legal position of Victorian women. J.W. Kaye's "Outrages on Women," *North British Review* 25 (May 1856): 233-56; Margaret Oliphant's "The Laws Concerning Women," *Blackwood's Edinburgh Magazine* 76 (April 1856): 379-87; and William Smith's "Infanticide," *Saturday Review* 2 (August 9, 1856): 335-36, provide a sense of the differing perspectives on women's often-overlapping roles as criminals and victims. Frances Power Cobbe, "Wife Torture in England," *Contemporary Review* 32 (April 1878): 55-87; C.A. Fyffe, "The Punishment of Infanticide," *Nineteenth Century* 1 (June 1877): 583-95; and Elizabeth Wolstenholme, *Infant Mortality: Its Causes and Remedies* (Manchester: A. Ireland, 1871), were uniformly pointed in their criticism of legal inequity and argued that the injustices created by the laws were actually increasing rather than decreasing criminal behavior. Cobbe also attacked the disparagement implicit in women's legal status in the article "Criminals, Idiots, Women and Minors: Is the Classification Sound?" *Fraser's Magazine* 78 (1868): 777-94.

The *Westminster Review* published a continuing critique of women's legal position between 1887 and 1905, including an article on judicial gender bias (149 [1898]: 50-62, 147-60) and a cogent discussion of misplaced chivalry, "Privilege versus Justice to Women," 152 (1899): 128-41. Arthur Rackham Cleveland's *Women under the English Law* (London: Hurst and Blackett, 1896) and Elizabeth Wolstenholme's *The Criminal Code in Relation to Women* (Manchester: n.p., 1880) are similarly articulate on the problems but more comprehensive than the individual articles. Annie Besant's *Sin and Crime: Their Nature and Treatment* (London: Freethought Publishing Co., 1885) adds a contemporary feminist perspective on the issue of holding women to a different, more rigid behavioral standard than men. In contrast, Sir James Fitzjames Stephen's voluminous contributions to the history of English law and the interpretation of modern legal practice made little comment on the legal distinctions between men and women except in discussing the punishment of infanticide.

Recent work that comments on Victorian women and the law within a historical frame of reference includes Alan Harding, *A Social History of English Law* (Baltimore: Penguin Books, 1966); Douglas Hay, "Criminal Justice in 18th and 19th Century England," in *Crime and Justice*, vol 2, ed. Norval Morris (Chicago: Univ. of Chicago Press, 1980); and J.J. Tobias, *Crime and Industrial Society in the 19th Century* (London: Batsford, 1967). More directly focused discussions are found in Barbara T. Gates, *Victorian Suicide: Mad Crimes & Sad Histories* (Princeton: Princeton Univ. Press, 1989), which was published after my manuscript was completed; C. Hall and N.E. Hull, *Murdering Mothers: Infanticide in England and New England, 1558-1803* (New York: New York Univ. Press, 1981); Joan Mannheimer, "Murderous Mothers: The Problem of Parenting in the Victorian Novel," *Feminist Studies* 5 (Fall 1979): 530-46; and Keith Thomas, "The Double Standard," *Journal of the History of Ideas* 20 (1959): 195-216. Gates and Mannheimer, like Philip Collins in *Dickens and Crime* (Bloomington: Indiana Univ. Press, 1968); Keith Hollingsworth, *The Newgate Novel, 1830-1847* (Detroit: Wayne State Univ. Press, 1963); Douglas MacEachen, "Wilkie Collins and British Law," *Nineteenth Century Fiction* 5 (1950): 121-39; and Paul C. Squires, "Charles Dickens as Criminologist," *Journal of the American Institute of Criminal Law and Criminology* 29 (1938-39): 170-201, relate legal history specifically to literary treatments of crime but not always exclusively to women.

Although his work is much broader in scope than my study and universally credited as a classic, I want to acknowledge the impact of

Michel Foucault's monumental *Discipline and Punish*, transl. Alan Sheridan (New York: Pantheon Books, 1978) on my ideas about literature's obsession with crime and punishment. I also want to mention several texts that influenced my methodology, both in linking literature to its social context and in thinking about women in literature and society: Flavia Alaya, "Feminists on Victorians: The Pardoning Frame of Mind," *Dickens Studies Annual* 15 (1986): 337-80; Roger B. Henkle, "New Work in the Study of Literature and Society: Applications for the Analysis of Nineteenth Century British Fiction," *Dickens Studies Annual* 14 (1985): 337-57; Jane Tompkins, *The Cultural Work of American Fiction, 1790-1860* (New York: Oxford Univ. Press, 1985); and several collections of essays on feminist criticism, especially Shari Benstock, ed., *Feminist Issues in Literary Scholarship* (Bloomington: Indiana Univ. Press, 1987); Ellen Carol DuBois, et al., eds., *Feminist Scholarship in the Groves of Academe* (Urbana: Univ. of Illinois Press, 1985); and Judith Newton and Deborah Rosenfelt, eds., *Feminist Criticism and Social Change* (New York and London: Metheun, 1985).

Finally, John Bender's *Imagining the Penitentiary* (Chicago: Univ. of Chicago Press, 1987) seems to me to set the standard against which all scholarship on the intellectual synergy of literature and criminal justice must be measured. He shows how the themes of eighteenth-century literature directly influenced the radically new approach to discipline and punishment exemplified in the emerging penitentiary system. His literary criticism and his social history are lucid and informed, and when he unites them he validates this rather unusual interdisciplinary field.

INDEX